GOD'S PRESENCE
Among the Aging

Fifty-five Meditations
a new series
Dealing with Stress

by
James E. McEldowney

First printing, 1982
Second printing, 1988

A Publication of
The Southmark Foundation on Gerontology
Bradenton, Florida, 1988

To my wife
Ruth Calkins McEldowney

Library of Congress Catalogue
Card Number 88 60655

Manufactured in the United States of America
Central Publishing Company, Inc.
Indinapolis, Indiana

CONTENTS

INSPIRATION FOR DAILY LIVING

PREFACE

"Spiritual well-being is the affirmation of life in a relationship with God, self, community, and environment that celebrates and nurtures wholeness." This definition, affirmed by more than 30-member religious denominations in the National Interfaith Coalition on Aging, is another way of stating that spiritual well-being is best experienced when we are aware of the presence of God.

To be fully human is to know Him in whose image we are made. In that presence, we can negotiate phenomenal stresses and joys, losses and opportunities because of the power and effect of God's presence on our individual situations. This fact is as true when we are young as it is when we are old. I find, however, that the changes associated with growing older have increased my awareness of God as a present and loving person in my life.

Whether this book is read by the individual or used to minister to others; the messages that follow flow from "the pen of a ready scribe." The prophet Isaiah said, "The Lord God has given me the tongue of him that is taught, that I may know how to sustain with a word him that is weary..." (Is. 50:4) Dr. McEldowney testifies in these pages to a life sensitive to the presence of God, and thus gifted with the sustaining word. The presence of the Lord, according to Acts 3:17, brings "times of refreshing" to the believer, whatever our experience, whatever our age, whatever our creed. That presence is central to spiritual well-being. In that presence this book of meditations comes alive with meaning.

Rev. Thomas C. Cook, Jr.
National Interfaith Coalition on Aging, Inc.

FOREWORD

There are numerous reasons why I, as a physician, have encouraged the publication of this book of meditations.

First, I recognize that is is very badly needed. Fifteen years of administering to the health needs of older patients in Bradenton, Florida, have underscored my belief that mental and spiritual strength are inseparably linked to physical well-being. We need to treat the WHOLE person. Experience has taught me a clear lesson: the healing powers of those who are at peace with themselves and with God are often miraculous. Viewed from the opposite perspective, I can attest to the fact that even the greatest "wonders" of medical science have limited benefit when the patient is spiritually anemic. As I guided the development of a chain of full-service retirement communities, I deliberately included in the plans for each project provisions for the ministry of a chaplain and for regular worship services to promote the spiritual health of our residents. The devotional messages in this book add another important dimension to this program; they help the readers spiritually and thereby add to their total well-being.

Second, I see a steadily increasing stress factor in the aging process. Each day, the number of retired citizens is increasing by 5,000. The individual needs, desires, and capabilities of retirees are getting progressively lost in the mounting "bureaucratization" both of governmental and private agencies—sometimes even in the "clinical" approach being used more and more by personal physicians. It is critically important for us to pierce the thickening veil of statistics and bureaucracy and to grasp the special situation of each person. Stress comes from many sources. Many are faced with financial catastrophe. Many are separated from spouses, families, and friends. Many are frustrated and perplexed regarding their most basic needs for comfort and security. This book will be a source of individual strength—badly needed in a climate of rising stress and insecurity. It is a source that will be constantly available and infinitely personal.

Third, I have enormous respect and admiration for Dr. James E. McEldowney, who is uniquely qualified in both professional training and personal experience to prepare this book. I have viewed first-hand his magnificent achievements as chaplain of the Shores, a retirement complex in Bradenton, Florida. I often wish it were possible to document statistically the outstanding contribution he has made to the welfare of the residents there.

Dr. McEldowney's background includes a Ph.D. in Historic Theology earned at the University of Chicago. His doctoral thesis was a fascinating account of the theological understanding of a whole line of Christians as they attempted to discover how God reveals himself to mankind. Then, for more than thirty years, he served as a missionary in India—first as a pastor, and later as professor of the Old Testament and an administrator. Subsequently he introduced and help organize the use of mass media in the life of the church. He served as Administrative Director of the World Association for Christian Communication in the Association's London offices; and in cooperation with church leaders in the South Pacific, he helped lay the foundation for Christian Mass Media that today links together people in the scattered islands of the region.

He began to think more seriously about the aging during a five-year pastorate in Virginia. He is outspoken among these older people who say they do not so much need things done for them as they want to use their storehouse of wisdom and experience creatively to help themselves and others.

I know of no one who is better able to prepare this book. Great spiritual strength is available to those who will but take time to read and absorb the meditations he has assembled.

Richard T. Conard, M.D.

INTRODUCTION

These meditations have been prepared with a twofold purpose in mind. Chaplains in retirement centers and other religious leaders will use them in their work with older people. Here are resources, challenging thoughts, insights, and spiritual understanding drawn from numerous sources that will enrich their ministry.

The book will have a still wider use. Individuals and groups will find in these pages inspiration and insights to help them develop spiritual lifestyles that express faith, hope, and love and relate them to the heart of God. Here are thoughts that will bring comfort and stimulate spiritual growth among those in retirement centers, in scattered homes, in hospital beds, or wherever older people are found.

We believe there is need for such a book. Changes among the aging in this generation must be recognized and spiritual insights applied. As a preparation for a broader understanding of these messages, we will note some of those changes and examine what is now spoken of as a "new philosophy of aging." But we also need to open our minds to the more positive and deeply spiritual ways to undergird the worth and dignity of those who are older. We need to rethink the love of God as it relates to them. But first, let us remind ourselves of the innovations that have so radically changed the lifestyle of those who are aging.

Toward a Philosophy of Aging

The most profound change in our social structure since the days of the frontier is the rapid increase in both the number and percentage of older people in the population. Within the past generation this important segment of society has been hedged about with new developments in our social structure that include Social Security, Medicare, adult communities and condominiums, nursing homes and hospices, together with Meals-on-Wheels, Congregate meals, and organized forms of extended care for the more isolated elderly. Most of these simply did not exist a generation ago.

ix

The need to implement these innovations has called into being a whole new set of organizations and agencies or has restructured existing ones. Government, churches, synagogues, private investors who erect new facilities, and others are involved. When addressing these new phenomena, people and organizations have made frenzied and experimental approaches, some of which have led to suffering and anguish; but mingled in the transition are gratifying islands of well planned care.

The aging, themselves, have been the ones most affected by this turbulence that marks a traumatic end of one era and the birth of a new. They have had to form new attitudes and new approaches to these changes.

Once, as parents grew older, they were drawn deeper into the tender care of the family. Today, with family life itself disrupted and fragmented, the aging are often moved to the fringe and become objects of pity. Many have been compelled to leave familiar haunts and friends and are asked to begin a new life at a time when their economic, physical, emotional, and social resources are stretched to the breaking point.

Within this changing environment, there are emerging distinctly new responses that may well give the elderly both greater security and also a higher status in tomorrow's social structure. Here are some of the core ideas of that philosophy.

1. Every human being has the right to live out his or her years in dignity. Each one must be able to approach his or her full potential during every level of change within the aging process, from independent living to full-time skilled nursing care, as changes take place.

2. The aging, themselves, must develop more positive responses so that the labels "inactive" and "senile" will no longer apply. They will experience a "second wind" for life. They will utilize their reservoirs of strength and participate in activities that help make these the best years of their lives.

They do this when they capitalize on physical, social, spiritual, and psychological changes that come with aging. Physically, they accept the emphasis on body fitness through exercise, lessening their dependence on medication. They participate in community affairs. They reawaken talents that have remained dormant for years. Spiritually, they draw on powers outside themselves to meet the worst that can happen to them. Psychologically, they develop healthy mental attitudes that undergird all of life.

3. Today's elderly, as well as the public in general, more readily accept physical aids such as canes, walkers, wheelchairs, hearing devices, glasses, and pacemakers. This changing attitude can be attributed in part to the exceptional use some of the more seriously handicapped have made of aids. A personal acceptance of such aids not only adds to mobility, but also has a positive psychological value.

4. A fresh understanding of the meaning of life has brought marked changes. Death is faced with greater realism. The almost mystical regard for the body after death is giving way to a greater recognition of the spiritual and eternal qualities of each unique personality that transcend the physical. This new attitude manifests itself in many ways, not the least of which is to call into question the use of life-support systems that merely prolong physical existence when all other responses have ceased.

There must, then, be a wholistic approach to aging. Wholeness of personality that gives dignity and quality to life is possible when the separate and combined needs of body, mind, spirit, and social outreach are recognized and promoted. In a similar way there is a wholistic concept of society that calls for interaction among the young, the middle aged, and older persons. As each contributes to the others, all share a fuller life. Wholeness, then, has to do with both the individual and society. When wholeness is taken into account it will contribute much to the later years of those who are older.

Toward a Meaningful Spiritual Experience

The objective of a spiritual ministry is to relate individuals and groups to the steadfast love of God in ways that stimulate healthy outlooks and enlarge responses—to not only transform life spiritually but also contribute to one's physical, intellectul and social well-being. The end result must be what Jesus spoke of as "the abundant life." Those in the older age-bracket are especially in need of such spiritual life-supports. We would do well to look at some of the spiritual affirmations that strengthen and undergird life.

1. We are endowed through creation with a spiritual nature that makes us uniquely able to communicate with God, our Maker. When God breathed into mankind the breath of life, man became a living soul. Our souls, our spirits are restless, as St. Augustine said, until they find their rest in God.

2. We are made in such a way that the more we live in tune with God's eternal purposes, the better able we will be to cope with life's problems, and the richer our experiences will be. This holds true not only for us as individuals but is fully as applicable to society. Love, kindness, and generosity give a heightened quality to both the individual and the group. Their opposites simply tear life apart. To respond positively is life-fulfilling and leads to spiritual and psychological maturity.

3. We need a more positive way to deal with human weakness than to focus on the terrors of sin. Saint Paul advises us to "overcome evil with good." (Romans 12:21b) The more completely we fill our lives with what is good and the more we actively cultivate a creative, positive, helpful, and loving attitude toward life, the purer our lives will be and the more radiantly happy we will become.

4. A spiritual quality permeates all of life. Our bodies are the temples of God, and we should not neglect nor dissipate them. Our minds must reach out to know the truth, for truth sets us free. No one is an island unto himself; the healthy person reaches out in service to others. Consequently, as we open the windows of our souls and seek to become spiritually One with the Eternal, even the turbulences and perplexities of life will become avenues of growth. We learn to breathe in and breathe out the spiritual strength God provides.

Our spiritual concerns come down to the basics. God is love. Our most important response is to open ourselves to "the drawing power of God's love," to use an expression of John Wesley. When we do this, it does not automatically free us from suffering, or pain, or an unfriendly environment; but as we experience God and rely on his power, he undergirds and comforts us so that at each moment, whatever our circumstances, we can meet life victoriously. There can be no more compelling evidence of God's presence than to witness a person who orders his or her life on this discovery. The love of God becomes the joy and strength of such a person both during this life and for all eternity.

The Broad Appeal Of This Book

The objective of a dedicated ministry is to relate every life to God. It is not a simple task to make God real to people of different backgrounds. There are the proverbial fifty-seven varieties of Protestants. And while I am a Protestant minister, my ministry must also include Roman Catholics, Orthodox, and people of the

Jewish faith. I must also remember all those who do not regard themselves religious, but who are equally in need of God's blessing. One can never be certain what triggers spiritual growth and turns life around, but one's ministry must have that as its goal. Possibly it is a mystical combination of faith, hope, and love. The emphasis will be on man's redemption and his spiritual fulfillment.

While I have been nurtured in the Christian tradition and owe so much to Jesus and his revelation of God, I have likewise been uplifted by spiritual giants within other religions and cultures. I have become profoundly aware of the mysteries of God at work in ways beyond my full understanding. I find that many of the Jewish faith look for a spiritual ministry to relate them to God. They challenge me to enrich and strengthen their faith and help them become sensitive to all God can do for them. I believe this was the essential motive behind what Jesus said and did—to relate the life of his day and our lives now and through all eternity to the Father, who was to him the God of Abraham, Isaac, and Jacob, of Moses, David, and the Prophets. In a unique way he shared their spiritual discoveries and purposes.

There is then a dominant theme running through these meditations. I want to relate each one to God as best I can, so the spiritual floodgates of life may be opened and spiritual lifesupports strengthened for the joy, comfort, and blessing of everyone who will let God nourish him or her. Eternal life does not begin after death. We are in the midst of it now.

Inspiration For Daily Living

I DARE YOU

John 15:12-27

There is something stimulating in a challenge. You may recall how, when you were young and someone said, "I dare you," you were almost sure to take the dare. The dares that come to you these days may be different. Some of you may be hearing a therapist dare you to get your muscles and mind fully functioning again. You are told to exercise until it hurts; so you start right in. Or you get on a three-wheeler, and round and round you go. There are other dares. Once again you take hold of a paint brush after years of neglect, and slowly the art begins to come back. One resident told me the other day, "I had real good hands once, but now they shake too much, so I am a volunteer to walk with people when they go for their exercise, or I run necessary errands for them." He went on, "It is amazing, there are some who let their problems get them down and they just sit. That would kill me (and he was more right than he realized). I have to get out and what a wonderful new experience I have had in meeting so many nice people as a volunteer." He had heard, "I dare you," and he had taken the dare.

Jesus was somewhat of a psychologist before psychology became academic. It must have seemed exceedingly strange when Jesus said to a girl caught in sin, "Neither do I condemn you, go and sin no more." He dared her to do right. He seemed to be saying that the cure for low appetites and the healing of many of the seemingly serious anxieties is to cultivate a taste for what enlarges, beautifies, and fulfills life. He didn't excuse sin. He didn't close his eyes to the devastating effects of sin. Rather he said, I dare you to respond to what is bigger and better. I demand sacrifice, goodness, kindness, and that you serve others, so that you might find a real life.

You have probably heard the legend of Ulysses. On his mythical voyage he passed the island of the Syrens, whose beautiful music

1

lured sailors to their death. To avoid this and pass the island safely, he stopped the ears of his sailors with wax. Then along came Orpheus. He, too, had to pass the island, but he didn't use wax. He created such inspiring music—music that was so commanding and vigorous—that the songs of the Sirens were as nothing in comparison.

There was a time when it was thought that the only way to be a good Christian was to close one's eyes to everything beautiful or challenging here on earth and sit morosely thinking of heaven. But when you search the Gospels, you find Jesus opening people's eyes. He unstopped their ears. We don't know how well he could sing, but on the night before the crucifixion, he and his disciples sang together in the Upper Room before they went out to the Garden of Gethsemane. He opened the eyes of the physically and spiritually blind, and he unstopped their ears, so both might discover the good and would not yield to the bad.

We see this ability to open up life superbly illustrated when he walked by the Sea of Galilee and called Simon Peter and his brother Andrew to leave their nets and follow him. James and John were there, too, and to them he said, "Leave off fishing. I dare you to become fishers of men."

This kind of daring-response action is at work in hundreds of ways in your lives. Some years ago, there was a television series called "Up and Down Staircase." In it a classroom was a riot of confusion; boys and girls brought their problems from the streets and their homes. Some of them even brought their knives. There was turmoil as they gave vent to their dislikes, prejudices, jealousies, and grudges. Because of their bitter fighting the learning process was impossible. Then something happened. The teacher introduced them to "The Tale of Two Cities." She got them involved in thinking and looking at others who were trying to handle life situations that were as complicated as theirs. She stimulated their imaginations. She made them think and when that happened, many of her pupils began to find themselves; the classroom confusion gave way to a real learning experience.

A good teacher dares her pupils to examine greater truths; and when this happens, the immediate problems take a back burner. The Apostle Paul spelled out a better way, "Overcome evil with good." (Romans 12:21)

Part of our problem may be that we respond to the wrong kind of dares—dares that degrade life rather than fulfill it. Those who turn to the bottle to drown out their problems gradually sink lower and lower. Jesus had a way to trigger good responses and when we take those kind of dares, our lives shape up. Even tired muscles can flex once more; though we may never again run and dance and sing as we once did, there is an exhilaration and joy in discovering the outer limits to our skills, our friendships, our spiritual growth.

Take another look at Jesus. Did you ever notice that he did not so much attack the major crimes of his day? There were highway robberies then. Jesus spoke of one such robbery when he told the story of the Good Samaritan, but the point of the story was not a condemnation of highway robbery, though of course it was wrong. Rather, he used the incident to say something important to all people. He pointed out how even good people such as a Priest and a Levite were so callous they did not go to the help of a victim of a crime. He indirectly condemned them because they shut their eyes to a man in desperate need. And ever since Jesus told that parable, the whole world has been struggling with larger questions, Who is my neighbor? What is my responsibility to him? From that moment these questions took on enlarged and terribly personal implications.

There was debauchery in Jesus' day—houses of ill fame, shameful social practices, and these are mentioned in such a fine story as the Prodigal Son. But again, the story is told not to denounce those social and very common sins, but he told of a boy who wasted his life doing what he thought would bring him fun, only to discover that it lowered him to the lowest on the scale of values. Then arrives the moment that he came to himself and he says, "I will arise." The story really turns on two moments of high experience: the first, when he struggles to his feet. He takes the dare to make something of himself. The other moment was when his father, who had been watching for him, runs to meet him and receives him home with forgiving love. The father took the dare to give his son another chance. And both of these high moments are a symbolic life pageant of redemption. God dares to take another chance with sinful men and women.

"I dare you." It may seem strange that I would suggest that possibly the most important thing you can do is to take a fresh look at yourself—to see yourself through spiritual eyes. Psychologists tell us that rarely, if ever, do we approach our full potential. Jesus seemed endowed with the skill to touch life in such a way he triggered responses that let loose the good, that made people dissatisfied with the ordinary and he encouraged them to strive for the best. What is

3

more, he took people where he found them—fishermen, tax collectors, a harlot, a thief on the cross, youth, old age, those who were well, those who were sick—and he dared them to open up their lives to God, and when that happened, you might say the butterfly emerged from the cocoon. And this has been the repeated experience of people like you and me for 2000 years. "I dare you." Give it a try.

"O LOVE THAT WILL NOT LET ME GO"

I Corinthians 13; Ezekiel 18.

We often draw comfort, guidance, and inspiration from rare souls who show that deep within the human breast are treasures of wisdom and understanding, of faith and compassion that speak to our need. Such inspiration has come to many through one of our most beautiful hymns.

O Love that will not let me go,
I rest my weary soul in Thee;
I give Thee back the life I owe,
That in Thine ocean depth its flow
May brighter, fairer be.

O Light that followest me all my way,
I yield my flickering torch to Thee;
My heart restores its borrowed ray,
That in Thy sunshine's blaze its day
May richer, fuller be.

O Joy that seekest me through pain,
I cannot close my heart to Thee;
I trace the rainbow through the rain,
And feel the promise is not vain
That morn shall tearless be.

O Cross that liftest up my head,
I dare not ask to fly from Thee;
I lay in dust life's glory dead,
And from the ground there blossoms red
Life that shall endless be.

4

This hymn is made all the more heartwarming when we learn the circumstances that led George Matheson to write it. What happened to him could have made him bitter and rebellious. Misfortune and heartbreak call out different responses in those who experience them.

During his days at the university he met a beautiful girl, and they planned to be married. Then his eyesight began to fail and his doctors informed him that he was going blind and they could not prevent it. He carried the sad news to his young lady who rather than sympathize with him, immediately broke off the engagement, declaring, "I do not want to be married to a blind man." Up until then she had shown him love, but when that love was tested, she had let him go.

Matheson finished his studies and was ordained into the ministry. The words of the hymn came to him on the eve of his sister's wedding. He had gone to assist in the ceremony; when he was alone in his room the night before the wedding, these words came in a flash of insight. He penned them and showed them to the family the next day. George Matheson did not permit his blindness to turn him from the ministry. He became one of the greatest preachers of England and was invited, in time, to preach before the Queen. Many who heard him did not realize he as blind.

The hymn is all the more inspiring when we consider that it was penned by a man who could not see. How unusual for one in constant darkness to reflect on the "light that followed" him all the way, as we read in verse two. Now there was inner light. He had yielded his flickering torch of physical sight to God, but good had come of it. "My heart restores its borrowed ray that in Thy sunshine's blaze its day may brighter, fairer be." God's inner light exceeded that of his most glorious days of physical sight.

He moved on to speak of joy—a joy that came to him through pain. Again this was visual, for his joy, like the rainbow, owed its brilliance to the dark clouds and the rain out of which it was formed. Joy, like beauty, lies hidden in the storm until God's light releases it. Matheson had seen the rainbow and it spoke to him of a joy born of suffering. Nor did his blindness shut out the outline of the cross, for to him the cross was a symbol of an endless splendor—of eternal life itself. Was his blindness a cross he must bear? Was his loss of the one he loved his special cross? Neither, for he writes of something more profound. There is no self pity here. He had discovered through his suffering a life and a love that gave his life new dimensions that would never end.

So Matheson had lost one love but he found another, and this new love would not let him go. It held him. It expressed itself in compassion, concern, a feeling of deep affection, a willingness to sacrifice.

The love Matheson wrote about is central in our religious heritage. All through the Psalms we read of the lovingkindness and mercy (the steadfast love) of God (See especially Psalm 136), and St. Paul writes of it most eloquently in his great love chapter. (I Corinthians 13) As you meditate on these expressions of love that will not let you go, you will turn the heartbreaks and perplexities of your lives into songs of rejoicing.

FILLING THE CUP OF LIFE

Genesis 28:10-22; Psalm 139:7-12

Anne Morrow Lindbergh made an inspired observation about the stories of the Bible. She said, "They are so simple, they are like empty cups for people to fill with their own experiences and drink for their own need over and over again, through the years."

Every Sunday School child has heard the story of Jacob and Esau. Jacob was the boy who stole his brother's birthright or blessing and then thought it best to run away until things cooled down a bit. How familiar that sounds. How often, as children or adults, we have done things we were ashamed of and then instead of setting things right, we run away—sometimes literally, we pack our bags and go away until things settle down. But more likely we just go into the next room, slam the door, and pout.

Jacob ended up at a place called Bethel. There, instead of a circle of friends he enjoyed at home, he was alone and in a strange place. There was no mother to feel sorry for him. We aren't told whether he had a morsel of food left, or whether he built a fire and made a hot drink, but we are told he tried to sleep. One problem was that he had forgotten his favorite pillow, and all he could find was a rock. That didn't sooth his spirits or quiet his fears. He turned and twisted, and when sleep finally came, he had a vision or a dream of angels

6

ascending and descending a stairway, and above all was God himself. He had thought that when he ran from home he had also run from God, for they didn't know then that God is everywhere. That vision really woke him up; and he said somewhat astonished, "God is in this place, and I knew it not." He had not run beyond God's care.

As Anne Lindbergh said, these Bible stories are like empty cups we fill with our own experiences and drink in time of need, time after time. This story is really saying to us, we can reach out and find God anytime, anywhere. Later one of the great psalmists was to put this in memorable words:

> Whither shall I go from thy Spirit?
> Or whither shall I flee from they presence?
> If I ascend to heaven, thou art there!
> If I make my bed in Sheol, thou art there!
> If I take the wings of the morning
> and dwell in the uttermost parts of the sea,
> even there thy hand shall lead me.
> If I say, 'let only darkness cover me,
> and the light about me be night,'
> even the darkness is as light with thee...
> How precious to me are thy thoughts, O God!
> How vast is the sum of them!
> If I would count them, they are more than the sand.
> When I awake, I am still with thee.
>
> (Psalm 139:7-12, 17, 18)

Can you recall a time when you wanted to run away?—to get away from the hurt or problem or situation that rose up to block you? And, at the very moment of crisis, you became aware that God was in that place and in that situation. It happens, possibly not often, but we do reach out, as Mrs. Lindberg said, and drink in his presence over and over again through the years. It may not happen only when you are running away. It can come in any moment of crisis.

Numerous stories in the Bible make us remember what has happened to us. There is something strangely familiar in the story of Abraham. He lived in Ur of the Chaldees. Then he felt a call to leave the familiar sights and sounds and go out into a strange land and among strange people; he went out trusting God, not knowing where he went.

That was my experience when I graduated from high school. The situation was further complicated, because it was the time of the depression in Iowa. Banks were failing and the future was grim. My eldest brother was already at college; and the brother just older and I were both scheduled to begin our college studies. The normal cost of any one of us at college was more than my father's entire salary in the churches he served.

To others it might have seemed hopeless, but my father had an implicit trust in God, and he had instilled in his family an awareness of God. Acting on this faith, he called us together and although he could not see what lay in the future, he said, "Get an education. The three of you boys rent a room. Cook your meals. We will bring what food we can. Borrow your tuition. We will start that way. We will go as far as we can. If we have to stop, we will; but we will go forward together with the help of God."

We did just that. We never had to stop. Before the end of the first year we discovered other boys who were having as hard a time as we. We brothers expanded our simple table to include as many as eight at a time before our three years together were finished.

As I look back on it, I cannot but believe God was in that place. We were able to go forward in faith and trust. The empty cup was filled, and we have drunk from it time after time as there was need.

Think back along the course of your life. Count the number of times you were afraid or alone and did not know how you could possibly go forward. You may be experiencing such a crisis just now. You may wonder how you can go forward. Much of the joy and blessing you have known has proceeded from earlier experiences of God's help in similar circumstances. At such moments you were aware that God was in that place and with his help you went forward. Rely on him now.

This meditation began with the story of Jacob at Bethel—alone, fearful, unable to escape from his problems. To his amazement God was there to quiet his fears and lead him forward. For us these Bible stories are like "empty cups for people to fill with their own experiences and drink for their own need over and over again, through the years," until as the psalmist says, "our cups run over." God's "goodness and mercy will follow us all the days of our lives." (Psalm 23)

8

SOMETHING TO HOLD ONTO

Isaiah 40:9-31

There are few people who do not experience traumatic losses at some time in their lives. We hear of heavy rains that send a river over its banks to sweep away the homes that families have put together, piece by piece, through their life times. Or a fire turns to ashes all their cherished possessions. Problems that we who are aging must face may be different, but they do not let us escape. We may lose the partner of a lifetime, or one or the other may be stricken by an incurable disease. The moment arrives when we must give up our home and move into what at first seems totally inadequate, cramped, and strange surroundings. Real and imaginary walls seem to close in on us, and life loses much of the familiar freedom and joy that gave us delight for so many years. The amazing thing is that when such things happen, it is truly possible to find something secure and entirely adequate to hold onto—something that is sufficient for the very worst that can happen to us.

A story is told of a village in a remote part of Europe where the people had been cut off from the cross currents of progress. It was the time when Haley's comet caused the skies to be filled with what appeared to be falling stars. In their remoteness, the people grew more fearful as every night the sky seemed to erupt with stars that were falling. Superstitions and questionable traditions added to their terror. It seemed that each one encouraged the next to be more fearful, until the village was almost overcome with panic.

The village minister became aware of their anxiety and was deeply troubled by their anguish. He called them together and said, "Don't look at the shooting stars. Look at the stars you know. Look at the north star and at Orion. See the fixed stars that have always pointed your way. They are there as they have always been. You have nothing to fear." Sure enough, as the villagers looked they saw the fixed stars—the stars they had always trusted; soon their panic was over. Once they had been reassured, they were able to take delight in the display of falling stars that came night after night, for they trusted their fixed stars.

Something like this can happen to individuals and even to nations to help us get ahold of ourselves. The Bible records many critical moments when the people of Israel went through periods of panic. In the course of years, they formed the idea that as long as the Temple in

Jerusalem stood they had nothing to fear; but the prophet Jeremiah warned them (chapter 7) that the Temple was not a fixed star and that even though it might fall it would not mean their end, but few listened. The time came when their Temple did fall, and for most of them all they could see was falling stars. With the destruction of Jerusalem in 587 B. C. by Nebuchadnezzar of Babylon, it seemed that everything had been lost, and they had reason to say so. Many of their leaders were taken in chains across scorching deserts to Babylon. Their sacred candle-sticks, the Ark of the Covenant and other Holy Vessels were carried away as booty. They were made to dwell as prisoners in a foreign land. Their sky was full of shooting stars, and they were in panic. To add insult to injury, the priests of Babylon taunted them; "Now where is your God? If your God were strong he would have protected you. Our gods are stronger. Your stars are falling."

The answer to their problem did not come at once; but in time there arose a prophet of the Exile, one we know as Isaiah, who told the people to look beyond their falling stars and fix their eyes once more on the steadfast love of Jehovah, their God. The fortieth chapter of Isaiah records how he pointed them once more to their fixed star, their powerful and majestic God, and his words are among the great messages of the Bible. His words of affirmation come down to us to remind us of the adequacy of our God to meet our most critical needs.

Get you up to a high mountain, O Zion, herald of good tidings.
Lift up your voice with strength. ... Lift it up, fear not. ...
Behold your God.
Your God is a great God.
He measures all the waters of the oceans in the hollow of his hand.
In a single span he reaches from horizon to horizon.
All the dust of the earth he gathers in his measuring cup.
The dust of all the mountains are like the dust left after weighing grain, on the scales.
Which one of the gods of Babylon has instructed God or given direction to the Spirit of the Lord?
Did any of their gods instruct him in justice or give him knowledge or understanding?
He, Jehovah, is your fixed star—your everlasting God, the Creator of the ends of the earth.
He does not faint or grow weary, his understanding is unsearchable.

He gives power to the faint
and to him who has no might he increases strength.
Even the youths shall faint and be weary,
And young men shall utterly fall;
But they who wait for the Lord shall renew their strength,
They shall mount up with wings like eagles,
They shall run and not be weary,
They shall walk and not faint.

(Adapted from Isaiah 40:9-31)

Here was something to hold onto; it gave even the faint-hearted new hope, so that in time they were able to go back and rebuild their fallen city.

The Lord our God is our fixed star. His steadfast love comforts us. Though all the falling stars of life surround us, we will not lose sight of our fixed star. Our faith and trust in God, the Father of our Lord Jesus Christ, holds us steady. God is our fixed star!

WINDOWS OF THE SOUL

Psalm 104, Luke 12:16-21

When we throw open the windows, take deep breaths of fresh air, turn and twist a bit to flex our muscles, our bodies are alerted and we really come alive. We do that spiritually when we worship. We throw open the windows of our souls, and through fellowship with each other we are prepared to meet life joyously. Such spiritual calisthenics has been put into a few lines of poetry I owe to the late Dr. Merton Rice of Detroit.

That the being in me may have room to grow;
    That my eyes may meet God's eyes and know,
I will hue great windows, wonderful windows,
    Magnificent windows, for my soul. (Author unknown)

We need to open the windows of our souls. We can get so involved in small matters that we neglect the important things in life. Jesus found this true of a certain man who spent his life accumulating wealth. He tore down his barns and built larger, and added to his

11

investments, piling up his wealth; and Jesus said, "Fool! This night your soul is required of you; and the things you have prepared, whose will they be?" Jesus added, "So is he who lays up treasure for himself, and is not rich toward God."

You and I concentrate on keeping our bodies trim, on satisfying our minds, on establishing friendships. We enjoy ourselves and live relatively care-free and self-satisfying lives. In some ways we give the impression we have made it. Then something happens. One in the family has a stroke, or health fails in other ways. Or we are threatened financially, and our world seems to collapse. At such a time we can almost hear those words, "Fool! tonight your soul will be required of you, then whose will these things be?" We then realize we lack the spiritual strength we so desperately need, and we begin asking ourselves how we can do what the poet has suggested—throw open the windows of our souls so we may see God's eyes and know.

How do we open the windows of our souls? That is the question John Wesley asked the Moravian, Peter Böehler, whose life seemed so perfectly related to God. Böehler said, "If you want to have faith, act as if you have faith; the time will come when you will act because you do have faith."

To feel God's presence in our lives we have to anticipate God. We have to act as if God were present; and, because we try to think what it would be like for God to be near, we begin to act, and lo! he is present. Consciously and unconsciously we have opened the windows of our souls.

You may remember the story of Byron's "Prisoner of Chillon." He was chained to a pillar in a dungeon. We might compare his bondage to ours, if we are chained to harmful appetites and if doubts and fears flood our minds. If we are devoid of spiritual graces, we are not free. One day the prisoner heard the song of a bird that came to him through a high window in his cell and the song set his life vibrating in a new way. That was a moment like our own when we begin to discover God's presence as he tells us there is more to life than the low form of life we have known.

The prisoner had a further experience. His brother who was chained near him, dies. In anguish he throws himself against his chains so powerfully that he breaks the chains. Now he is free to move about his cell. He digs a foothold in the wall so he can look out the window; and he now sees a whole new world—the eternal snows on the mountains, the clouds in the sky, an island with three tall trees and many flowers. Even the fish in the water outside his cell seem to wear a smile. He has opened the windows of his soul and a whole new vista, a whole new view of life opens to him. There is beauty and wonder. There is the magnificence of God's world. Spiritual discoveries can do that.

The day comes when the prisoner of Chillon walks free. The windows at last are opened, and he breathes the air of freedom. We can expect that when we open the windows of our souls.

How do we open the windows of our souls? The Bible is filled with soul-opening windows of God. Read again the 104th Psalm and let your soul stretch a bit. Regular reading of the Bible is a good beginning.

A further discipline is meditation. As you read, ask God what he is trying to say through each reading. Truth seems to pop out when we meditate. Note the poet's words, "great windows, wonderful windows, magnificent windows." We should expect to grow in spiritual understanding. Our world is flooded with hundreds of sects and cults founded by people who thought, when they had discovered one truth, that they had found it all. Through disciplined meditation and receptive listening to God we must continue to search for God's perfect will for us.

The practice of prayer is another window. Many excellent books of prayers are available to help us. No prayer has been of greater inspiration to me than this beautiful collect:

Almighty God, unto whom all hearts are open, all desires known, and from whom no secrets are hid; cleanse the thoughts of our hearts by the inspiration of thy Holy Spirit, that we may perfectly love thee, and worthily magnify thy holy name; through Christ our Lord, Amen.

Bishop Wescott opens another window with this prayer:

O Lord God, in whom we live, and move, and have our being, open our eyes that we may behold Thy Fatherly presence ever about us. Draw our hearts to Thee with the power of Thy love. Teach us to be anxious for nothing, and when we have done what Thou hast given us to do, help us, O God our Savior, to leave the issue to Thy wisdom. Take from us all doubts and mistrust. Lift our thoughts up to Thee in heaven, and make us to know that all things are possible to us through Thy Son our Redeemer. Amen.

Good as all such prayers are, they only wedge open the windows until we relate all this directly to life. It is in service that the windows of the soul are most perfectly opened.

Brother Lawrence, a monk, who lived in the 17th century learned this. He went to the chapel to pray. He sang hymns. But it was in the kitchen when at work he began to practice the presence of God, as he peeled potatoes, washed pots and pans, or trained a subordinate to work with him. The kitchen was where he needed God most, and God opened the windows of his soul until everyone thought of Brother Lawrence as one who practiced the presence of God in his kitchen. He made the discovery that he was closest to God, not on his knees, but when he was serving his fellow man.

Who can open the windows of his soul? Today's housewife in her kitchen, a husband and wife in their apartment, a craftsman at his machine, a lonely person in a hospital bed. And you, too, can open the windows of your soul.

Edna St. Vincent Millay has her way of saying this for me.

> The world stands out on either side
> No wider than the heart is wide;
> Above the world is stretched the sky
> No higher than the soul is high.
> The heart can push the sea and land
> Farther away on either hand;
> The soul can split the sky in two,
> And let the face of God shine through.
> But East and West will pinch the heart
> That cannot keep them pushed apart;
> And he whose soul is flat—the sky
> will cave in on him by and by.

THINK ABOUT IT

Philippians 4:8, 9.

The Apostle Paul reminded people of his day that there are some things you ought to be thinking about; and right from the beginning of this meditation I would ask you to think on these things. Paul wrote, "Whatever is true, whatever is honorable, whatever is just, whatever is pure, whatever is lovely, whatever is gracious, if there be any excellence, if there is anything worthy of praise, think about these things." Those who do this let positive thinking control their lives, for Paul advises that we make it a habit to dwell on these things, as he did, and they had become so much a part of his life he was able to add, "What you have learned and heard and received in me, do; and the God of peace will be with you."

Paul said, "Think on these things." Our minds are filled with a continuous parade of thoughts, and we cannot turn our minds off, even when we want to. Often after sleep comes, we have the bonus of dreams. Because in our waking moments something continually occupies our minds, we should follow Paul's advice and be certain our thoughts are positive and creative.

A negative thought that can truly annoy us is to hold a grudge. We fail to realize that holding a grudge doesn't really hurt the other person seriously, but it harms us every time we think about it. We should turn such matters over to God and forgive as fully as possible. Life is too great and too important to remain in bondage to low and miserable grudges. Paul said, "Think on these things."

Sometimes our minds dwell on trivial or evil things. The opposite of what Paul talked about is often highlighted in the news because violence, murder, rape, drugs—the morally obnoxious and somewhat vulgar—are made to appear sensational and get public attention. What happens for the community's good seldom involves a crisis situation. Paul would not have us ignore things that are evil, but it would be harmful for the mind to dwell on them or take delight in anything that adds horror to life. Paul encourages a healthy mental and spiritual habit. Select wholesome and generous thoughts that give a positive quality to one's total personality and make this a habit. "Think on these things."

Paul starts out by saying, think on whatever is true. Jesus taught, "Know the truth and the truth will make you free." (John 8:32) Much of life's tragedy comes when we feel that the truth is being covered up

15

or twisted. Yet, often we really do not want to know the truth, if knowing it would put demands on us. Are we prepared to know the whole truth about brutality, injustice, unemployment, and a denial of basic human needs? Would those engaged in the drug traffic or in crime, want others to know the truth? The denial of truth brings untold suffering to innocent people.

Our minds seem restless in a pursuit of truth. Yet it is healthy to pursue it and fill our minds with it. Any religion that cannot bear the scrutiny of truth is, of course, a false religion. All the time in our pursuit of truth we have the hope that we may see things exactly as they are. We must realize that we are subject to human limitations so the most even the best of us can know is only a fraction of what is held in the mind of God. That was one reason Jesus told his followers they must be like little children—teachable—and not have closed minds. The positive side of the matter is that the pursuit of truth can put a soul into a most joyous and exciting life, and this helps us understand what Paul had in mind. To dwell on high things of life is to crowd out whatever is low and mean. Why should we, with only one life to live, be content to crawl in the gutters of the mind when it is possible to attain the heights. Think on truth.

Here is a bit of truth as I have found it. Let your minds toy with it in the coming days. God is good. Life is made for goodness. When good triumphs, there is harmony. When we drive out jealousy and selfishness, then we are happy. We are made that way. Best of all, we make others happy, too.

Because we live in a society that bring us close together it would be well to give thought to another matter. We are all very different. We have our likes and our dislikes. We could get on each other's nerves if we did not avoid doing things or saying things that agitate others. Because we love those about us, we bring ourselves under control. We seek to please them. We apply the golden rule: "Do unto others as you would have them do unto you." That is a truth big enough to keep us busy for a long time.

But what do these further words of Paul stand for in your life? "Whatever is honorable, just, pure!" These are rugged and demanding, calling for strength and force of character. "Lovely, gracious, excellent, worthy of praise!" Here are stirring emotions, the warmth, the fine up-reach of the soul and heart that makes us worthy of praise. How different all life would be if these were to dominate our lifes and if we were to fix our minds on them.

All these belong together. As Paul said, "Think on these things. Whatever is true, whatever is honorable, whatever is just, whatever is pure, whatever is lovely, whatever is gracious, if there is any excellence, if there is anything worthy of praise, think on these things."

LOW SPIRITS

Psalm 42, Isaiah 26:3

As with many others, I sometimes experience what I would call for lack of a better term, "low spirits." Once it came just after Easter. In some ways I had been on a mountain top experience during Holy Week but I had to come down, even as Jesus and disciples did from the Mount of Transfiguration. While they had been on the Mount, Simon Peter had declared that Jesus was the Messiah, the Son of the Living God. Peter had come down from that experience and when he was at the trial of Jesus, in a moment of weakness he had said, "I never knew him." Afterwards he went out and wept bitterly. Low spirits seem to come to the best of us. Even such a great poet as Thomas Gray once said, "Low spirits are my true and faithful companions. They get up with me and go to bed with me, make journeys and return when I do." And George Elliot had her low spirits. "My address is Grief Castle, on the River Gloom, in the Valley of Sadness."

It isn't exactly strange that low spirits come, but it would be a strange and terrible thing if we did nothing about them. The psalmist asked, "Why are you cast down, O my soul? and why are you disquieted within me? Hope in God, for I shall again praise him, my help and my God."

Dr. Norman Vincent Peale of New York tells about a man he met in Switzerland. Mr. Flukmann was 84 years of age and had lived a rugged, difficult life in the mountains. He had to drive his cattle to high pasture in the summer and bring them to the valley for the winter. Dr. Peale looked at the old, twisted, hardy man and said, "Mr. Flukmann, you impress me as a very happy and contented man. Why are you that way? You do not seem to be troubled by anything."

Flukmann replied. "True, I am contended. I do not have hardly anything but that does not worry me because I haven't much to lose. I have a strong body. I can eat simple food. I don't let things bother me because I trust in God." He added, he was like the psalmist of old who had said, "Though I walk through the valley of the shadow of death, I fear no evil, for thou art with me."

Dr. Peale returned to New York and it was not long before he met a man who was about the same age as Mr. Flukmann, but this man began to complain. He had a bad leg, he was on a diet, he did have lots of money but, he asked, "What good is money, if I am miserable?"

Dr. Peale told him about Mr. Flukmann and how happy he was in Switzerland because he put his trust in God. The man in New York belonged to the Jewish faith so Dr. Peale reminded him what Isaiah the prophet had said, "Thou will keep him in perfect peace whose mind is stayed on thee."

Our trouble is we let disturbing things fill our minds. Any one of us could find enough wrong to make us miserable. One day as I sat down to type out two prayers to use in a service, I felt pain in one of my fingers. The day before while working in the yard I had broken two fingernails down deep, and when I touched the typewriter they pained me. But I said, "I can take it. What is a little pain, anyhow?" I shut the thought of pain out of my mind and finished my typing. When I put away bad thoughts and chose to put my mind on what might be of help to others, the pain was eased.

We must tune our thoughts to God's thoughts. One writer lived in a high building in New York. When he looked out all he could see were walls—walls of buildings all around him. He said, "I've lost my horizons." When our minds are stayed on God, we do not allow our "low spirits" to close out our horizons. We are lifted up, even as the psalmist said, "Why are you cast down, O my soul? Why are you disquieted with me? Hope in God, for I shall again praise him, my help and my God."

Join me now in one of the prayers I typed with my painful fingers.

Eternal God, the utterance of your name hushes me and makes me humble. The thought of your creation tempers me with awe. The contemplation of your forgiveness makes me marvel at your tender mercy. Life is filled with so many mysteries. There is so much we do not understand, but because we can feel your love we seek to find you. At times we are beset with doubts and fears;

and we know despair. We are tormented by jealousies, suspicion, anger, and anxiety. But when we turn to you at such moments, we throw open our lives for your guidance and blessing. So bend our wills to yours that we may know fullness of life and may be among those who give utterance to every helpful thought and act that lets us share the abundant life. In Jesus' Name, Amen.

EXPERIENCING GOD

Psalm 98

In India, a group of students and I once walked across the fields to a remote village where we had been told a man lived who claimed to be God. We went, not because we expected to see God in the flesh, but to have a look at a man whom the villagers deified.

We came at last to his somewhat broken-down, mud hut. He was clothed as other villagers in a loin cloth and was performing what appeared to be a rite or ceremony over the frail body of a tiny baby. The mother, tense and silent, watched his moving hands, hoping for a cure this man obviously could not accomplish. We watched for a time, but the students decided that whatever other qualities this man possessed, he was not God; so we retraced our steps without a divine encounter.

What is God really like? Is it right to conclude, as one boy did, "I do not believe in God for I have never had an experience of him." Or is he, as he seems to be for some, a bit like a savings account, to be used only in an emergency? Upon what do we base our understanding of God?

The man Job, in the Old Testament, could not at all understand why God visited him with so many troubles. Job had not only lost all his possessions but also his family. Then he lost his health and was covered with sores. His wife advised him, "Curse God and die." But Job would not, for God was the only secure thing he could hold onto. He could not understand why he suffered; but his confidence in God's goodness did not waver and he said, "Though he slay me, yet will I trust him." He was certain that, long after he was gone, God's justice and wisdom would control human experience of each succeeding generation.

I would like to share with you certain convictions about God that have come to me through a life-time of experience. I have found these evidences helpful.

First, Jesus lived the most perfect and obedient life we have ever known. Yet, even this Son of God and Son of Man was crucified and died a shameful death. But even in death he reached out and laid hold of God, saying much like Job, "Father, into thy hands I commend my spirit." Jesus understood God as no other who has ever lived. He put himself in God's hands. I want to, too. We can see the results. Jesus has had the greatest influence for good in the history of humanity. I want him to guide my life. When I think of Jesus, somehow, I come immediately into the presence of God.

Second, my failures are not due to failures on God's part. My failures occur because I do not do even what I know is right. When I rely on him most I am best able to reach those goals of Christian conduct I have set before me. When I do this I experience the effective power of God in my life.

Third, I find that life is made for goodness. If life were made for sin or evil, then when we are jealous and hateful, selfish and brutal, life would be normal. If we were made that way and that were written into the laws of life, then an evil kind of life would fit together like a jig-saw puzzle. But these ugly forms of behavior do not fit. They make life miserable. They destroy life. Sin is not naturally helpful, it is not the highest good, humanly speaking; rather, sin is the terror of life. It is our enemy. But note, the opposite is true. We find our true selves when we are filled with love. We are made so that both we and society are fulfilled when love rules. This is a further evidence of God.

Fourth, in the second chapter of the Acts of the Apostles, we find a group of disciples hidden in an upper room, fearful, dejected, defeated. Their leader had been crucified. Then something happened. They were filled with power—overwhelming power from God—that completely changed them. God took those unlettered and simple men and women and made them fearless campaigners. A new breath of power flowed from Calvary, a breath that became a mighty wind and changed the course of history. They knew it as the power of God through Jesus Christ.

What is God like? When Albert Schweitzer tried to describe who Jesus is he wrote these words, "He comes to us as One unknown, without a name, as of old, by the lake-side, he came to the men who knew him not. He speaks to us the same word: 'follow thou me,' and sets us to the task which he has to fulfill for our time. He commands. And to those who obey him, whether they be wise or simple he will reveal himself in the toils, the conflicts, the sufferings, which they shall pass through in his fellowship, and, as an ineffable mystery they shall learn in their own experience who he is."

I trace back my understanding of God to a whole company of witnesses. There were Sunday-School teachers; ministers of the Gospel, of whom I put my father high on the list; devout professors; but chiefly ordinary men and women who have demonstrated that the secret of their lives has been the power of God at work in them. They lived far beyond their resources and their powers. In them, and in others, I have found God walking beside me to enlarge my vision and perform his redeeming purposes in my stubborn clay. Though I cannot explain why or how he seeks me out to give me his blessing, the evidence comes unmistakably every day. My redeeming God and yours surrounds us with his love as he fills us with his Spirit. Though much about God will always remain a mystery, we can experience much for ourselves. And our greatest experiences come as he releases his power and his love in us so that we can be a blessing and a guide to others, now and always.

Reach out in expectation and lay hold of him. He waits for you at every crossroad of life. "Let your heart take courage; yea, wait for the Lord!" (Psalm 27:14)

WHAT DOES LOVE LOOK LIKE?

1 John 4:7-12

I found a very old description of what love looks like in a book the other day. The description was written by St. Augustine who lived between 354 and 430 A.D., so it comes from the early centuries of Christianity. But it is so contemporary, I must pass it on to you, just as I found it.

To the question, "What does love look like?" Saint Augustine wrote,

It has the hands to help others.
It has the feet to hasten to the poor and needy.
It has the eyes to see misery and want.
It has the ears to hear the sighs and sorrows of men.
That is what love looks like.

Love becomes visible when we see it in living people. I discovered such love when I met George and Elsie Garden in Hyderabad, India. They lived and worked in the Methodist Boys' High School, which had been founded by their good friend John Patterson. It was Elsie's special joy to greet new students each year. Many came from remote villages to a strange city, to spend nine months in a boarding school. Though it was called a high school, it included children who were just beginning their education.

When Elsie met them she had to assure them that though they were away from home, they could count on her. She was someone in that strange and terrifying place who loved them and would do her best to be a mother to them. Some were almost paralyzed with fear until Elsie took a few at a time and got them to tell something about their village. Then she would get them to act out what was most amusing in their villages. Almost every Indian child is a born actor. Before long the ice was broken, and they lost their fear and were among friends, who, like themselves, were eager to learn. Best of all, they had found one who cared.

Elsie had ways to reach right into the lives of those boys. She could discover potential for music or drama or art or skills using their hands. She drew me into the circle when she asked me to form a boy's choir, that in time sang stirring music. One boy of that choir was later to take special training under my supervision, and today he carries on the work in Christian Communications that for a time was my specialty. Another of those boys is now one of the Bishops of his church, after being for a time Youth Secretary of the World Council of Churches in Geneva. If you were to ask either of them who helped them come alive to the possibilities of Christian growth, they would tell you, as they have told me many times, George and Elsie Garden.

George worked somewhat behind the scenes raising money, erecting new buildings, helping the school fit into the changing social patterns of India. There were some misfits among the students who just couldn't make it. I remember one in particular who had a serious handicap. He was deaf and had never learned to talk properly. He was just a problem to most of his teachers, but George had the patience and love to work with him year after year, helping him mature from a crippled, little boy to a graduate able to take his place in the world.

I saw that love tested, too, but it triumphed. Jealousies arise even in Christian circles, and there were some who coveted the positions of leadership the Gardens enjoyed. They finally had their way, and the Gardens were sent to a rural school that had never taken root in an impoverished part of the State. There were tears and anguish and possibly a trace of resentment at first. Neither felt called to shift overnight from the heart of a thriving city to a remote, rural school more than a mile from Zaheerabad, the closest village.

But the people of the countryside opened up to receive them. George began a study of soils and the problems of the farmers; within five years, he had almost doubled the yield in many of the fields— fields that were to grow the grain to feed the children in the school. Farmers from miles around would come to learn his secrets, and a whole new life opened up to George. He accepted the change from city to village in a spirit of love and let love work out through his hands and feet, his ears and eyes, That is what love looks like.

Their love spread through the countryside and word of the amazing things they were doing reached their homeland. It was decided that their story should be told on film; and a film team, together with script writers, came to Zaheerabad to tell their story. They came expecting to find a quiet, motherly woman surrounded by a circle of ordinary school-children. Before a day passed she spirited them with an amazing enthusiasm such as they had never known. Before they had come, they had sketched the outline of their story; but both Elsie and George opened up to them new dimensions of the story that made it come alive. They didn't have to concoct a story. They set their cameras running, and the story of the Garden's love unfolded. The Gardens were their inspiration and their story.

After more than 45 years of missionary service they retired to Nashville. Five years later they were invited back to see once more the work to which they had given their lives. Word spread that they were coming; and at every village along the railway line their former students and friends crowded near the train to see them and cover them with garlands of flowers. The love they had shown was being returned.

Then, some time ago, I had a phone call from George. "Elsie is in heaven," he said. Her arthritis had crippled her for many years, even before she returned from India, and her weakened heart finally gave out. St. Augustine told what love looked like more than 1500 years ago. That is still the way love looks today.

LIFE'S MEMORABLE MOMENTS

Acts 7:55-8:1, 9:4; Numbers 6:24-26

Earlier or later in life everyone should look forward to memorable moments when life takes on new meaning. It may be a sweeping religious experience such as John Wesley, founder of Methodism, had at an Aldersgate meeting. For some years he had been longing for such a trust in God that would assure him God had accepted him and would use his ministry to take religion out into the highways and byways of his beloved country. The moment of assurance came. His heart was "strangely warmed." This experience changed his life and we see his imprint on a growing circle of people ever since.

Another who had a memorable experience was Saul of Tarsus. During his youth he looked on the followers of Jesus as enemies of his faith, for he was a devout Jew. He was so passionately opposed to them that he went from city to city hunting them out so he could give them over to the authorities for trial. Then one day, he stood by while a mob surrounded one of the Christians, a man by the name of Stephen. Stephen had said things that the Jews felt had discredited their traditions. The mob dragged Stephen out to stone him. Members of the mob laid their garments at Saul's feet. Then Stephen knelt and prayed, "Lord, Jesus, receive my spirit. .... Lord, do not hold this sin against them." That was a moment Saul was to remember. Only a few days later, when he was on his way to Damascus, he heard a voice ask, "Saul, Saul, why persecutest thou me?" Things continued to happen until Saul the persecutor became Paul the evangelist. That memorable moment started a chain reaction among the early followers of Jesus that turned Christianity into a movement that swept across the Roman world.

Life has such moments—moments that change our whole lives—that bring rapture and joy and triumph.

You may ask, "What makes a moment memorable?" And further, "Are memorable moments reserved only for those who seem destined to change the world?" What about you and me?

The fact is most people who experience them are just ordinary people. There were few who expected Sadie Virginia Smithson of Johnson Falls, West Virginia, to have what later would be called a memorable experience. Dr. William Stidger, one of my professors, passed on the story he heard about Sadie that suggests that memorable experiences usually come when very ordinary people act in an extraordinary way in a moment of opportunity. That was certainly true of Sadie.

It was said that Sadie lived "on the wrong side of the tracks," for as she grew up she learned the bitter fact that the social set at school did not think she was good enough to belong to their Laurel Literary Society, which was a symbol of acceptance in their small community. Her father ran the livery stable (that dates the story), and she added to the family income by her sewing. Like many others when something is denied them, she got all upset and vowed, one way or another she would break the barrier and show the others just how good she was. Then she made her plans. She would save all she could and make a trip to Europe, for that was what the privileged people did; when she returned, everyone would listen as she read her paper on "My trip to Europe." Then they would be glad to make her a member of their society.

She scraped and saved and at last got to Europe, travelling with a professor and his family. As they went through Paris they had to leave one of the girls who was sick but the rest went on to Belgium. They had hardly arrived there when war was declared. Immediately the family and Sadie started back to Paris to be near the sick child. They had not gone far when they drove right onto a battlefield, soon after the fighting had moved on. Soldiers were lying all about where they had fallen. One, who had a terrible wound in his side, called out, "Water, for God's sake." It was more than Sadie Virginia Smithson could bear. She jumped out of the car, ran to a nearby spring, filled her little cup and took water to the dying man. Then she was overwhelmed by cries of other soldiers for water. The professor ordered her back in the car, but she refused, and at last the family drove on without her.

That was the beginning of an afternoon and night that changed her life. First it was to fill her cup with water. Then she took strips of clothing from her skirt and used them as bandages. She wrote notes for some of the boys and tramped among them until she was almost exhausted. The only thing that kept her sane was when she began to sing little ditties and songs she had known as a child. And as she left each one she would say, "God bless us and keep us, and make his face to shine upon us."

All night long she stayed on her feet, and with the coming of day, up the road came an ambulance. The young doctor got out and asked, "Who are you, and what in thunder are you doing here?"

As she looked around, she said, "I'm Sadie Virginia Smithson, and I've been holding hell back all night."

As the doctor looked around he could see what she had been doing. "Well," he said, "Miss Sadie, I'm glad you held some of it back, for everybody else in the world was letting it loose last night."

Then later, as she told her story, she said she had never had children of her own, but "all those men were my children, even the biggest and roughest of them. I believe I could have died for any one of them. I reckon being so crazy with pity has stretched me out of being a scary old maid into being a mother."

Someone asked whether she ever became a member of the Laurel Literary Society, and she answered, "You don't understand. I've been face to face with war and death and hell and God. I've been born again. Do you reckon any of them little old things matter now? Nothing but God and love and doing things for folks." Sadie's moment had changed her life.

But what about us? There are no such opportunities for us here. It is a matter of opening our eyes to see what is right around us. An experience that came to my wife and daughter helps confirm this. They were spending the summer in Kashmir, and had gone to

26

Palgam, high up in the Himalayas. There, a doctor ordered my wife not to travel the long return journey home lest she lose a second baby, for she was pregnant. They were living in a tent, in a circle of other tents of missionaries on vacation. Then the rains came; some days it rained so hard they did not venture out. This was especially boring for a child. My wife dredged up one story after another from her childhood in Iowa, to entertain Betty. Once, as she finished a lively account, Betty began to cry; and her mother asked the reason. "O Mother," she said, "You have had so many wonderful things happen. I will never live in Iowa, so I'll never be able to tell my children about such wonderful things."

There she was, in Kashmir, the roof of the world. She was surrounded by fields of mountain flowers. The snows and glaciers surrounded her. The sound of the flute and the call of shepherds echoed from one mountain to another. Years later she was to realize what memorable moments those were as she shared her time in Kashmir with her own children.

We never arrive at a place in life where there are no ingredients of memorable experiences. We have to use our imagination and recognize them and let the joy and excitement of the moment build up in us. As we discover the radiant meaning of many ordinary things around us, the ordinary becomes memorable; and our lives are refreshed and made glad. In worship, in organized games, in voluntary service, extraordinary things happen. The very way some who are severely handicapped handle life day after day, becomes a memorable experience for others.

Sadie said to the soldiers, "God bless us, and keep us, and make his face shine on us." With such a prayer we can turn the ordinary into a memorable moment.

THE POOR IN SPIRIT

Matthew 5:3

There is something awe-inspiring and deeply reverential when we meditate about God in an unusual place, whether it be a mountain top or on the shores of a lake or possibly just with an intimate group out under the stars. Jesus gave many of his teachings in such places. Matthew records what has become known as the Sermon on the Mount. It had more than a high hill for its setting; for in the fifth to seventh chapters of Matthew's Gospel, Jesus opened up people's minds to spiritual vistas that had strong moral and social overtones.

At the beginning of this Sermon we find the Beatitudes which have inspired generations of Christians. They are challenging precepts of the Christian life. Today we are to meditate on the first of the Beatitudes, "Blessed are the poor in spirit for theirs is the Kingdom of Heaven."

Jesus was speaking to a company of people who had come for inspiration and help. In the crowd that day were farmers and shepherds who had come from their fields because they had heard of this remarkable teacher. Women had left the grinding of their grain and the baking of their large flat loaves of bread. As they came across the fields they danced and sang in a holiday mood. Now as they sat together, some were nursing their babies. And there must have been children there also, for Jesus had said, "Let the children come to me. ... for to such belong the Kingdom of Heaven." (Mark 10:14) This beatitude applied especially to children because they were "poor in spirit"—teachable—so the Kingdom of Heaven would be theirs.

Priests and rabbis had also come to hear what Jesus had to say. Not all of them were prepared to respond kindly to his mystic power. Some hoped to hear words or discover some weakness they could later use to condemn him.

His mother was probably there, too, and some of the other women who heard him gladly. He had started them thinking that womanhood was included in the blessing of God. When they went to the Temple they could not go into the inner courts, for those were reserved for men. But here on the mountainside there were no lines of separation. Here they could receive the divine favor of God and learn about the blessed life of which Jesus spoke.

No wonder Jesus, when he looked out on eager faces, was moved with compassion, and that compassion broke the silence with the word, "blessed." When a Hebrew father put his hand of blessing on his son, something of the greatness of the father rubbed off onto the son—something of his long life and his inmost nature and character. And here was Jesus saying "blessed." He was saying that something of the essence of God would rub off on those who were poor in spirit. They would receive a divine favor and benefit that would lead to spiritual well-being. The poor in spirit, when they received this blessing, would become members of the Kingdom of Heaven and this Kingdom, as Jesus described it, pertains both to this life and to eternity.

It is not of little consequence that each of the beatitudes begins with the word "blessed." Those who receive into their lives the qualities spoken of in the beatitudes have the favor of none other than God himself. They cannot in their own power do any one of those things that make them blessed, but because of the mystical touch of God they can become, or then can do, all that Jesus speaks of in these sayings.

In India I have seen a form of blessing that has profound meaning. The word "darshan" signifies what happens when a disciple of a great religious leader bows before his "guru" or "enlightened one" to seek his blessing. It is a mystical moment when the disciple feels transfused with something of the greatness of the other. This power to bless is sometimes seen in great and respected leaders who have a force of character that can be felt by others. Mahatma Gandhi was such a one. When he reached out to touch them or even when he lifted his hand in blessing from a distance, they seemed to experience something of his greatness. The blessing almost transformed them so they were prepared to pursue their struggle for freedom no matter what sacrifice was demanded of them. For multitudes it was really a sacred moment. They received his blessing.

When Jesus spoke these beatitudes he touched the minds and hearts of the multitude in ways that were to make a difference. It was as if he were saying, God's spirit rests on those among you who are poor in spirit—you who know your limitations, you who are teachable, you who are ready to open your lives to what God wants to do through you. The very Kingdom of Heaven and all this implies will be yours, for you are ready to receive what God wants to do in and through you.

So Jesus was saying something like this, "You haven't begun to see

29

what God has in store for you, nor will you until you open your lives fully to God's love." So often we hold on to our doubts and prejudices. We judge each other by what we see each other do when we really do not know what is in the other person's mind or heart, or what pain or heartbreak may cause the person to act as he does. It is when we are truly poor in spirit that we make it possible for God to make us rich in understanding and in love. This can happen when we throw open our lives to receive God's blessing. The key is that we should be receptive to what God wants to do for us. Then we become the blessed ones—a blessing to everyone.

What a beginning for the Sermon on the Mount. Jesus called them to open wide the doors of their hearts and minds so God could sweep away sin and give them the blessing of the abundant life through his love. The Kingdom of God would be theirs when that happened.

BLESSED ARE THOSE WHO MOURN

Matthew 5:4

W hen Jesus said, "Blessed are those who mourn for they shall be comforted," there were, no doubt, many on the mountain side who asked, as you or I might, "Just what does he mean? How can those who mourn be comforted, and how does this make them blessed?" We are not normally attracted to persons who wear a mournful look or who speak in mournful tones, so we might ask, "Why did Jesus call them blessed?"

We would remind ourselves that in Jesus' day people filled the word "blessed" with rich meaning. When a father blessed his son, something of the essence or divine spark of the father passed from the father to the son. The blessing of God implies that something is received directly from God. In this case, that something takes away the depth of sorrow and brings comfort to the heart. So when those who mourn open their lives to receive the blessing of God, they are filled with comfort.

The word comfort, likewise, is full of meaning. The core idea is **fort** or to fortify. A fort immediately suggests strength, the ability to defend, and it also speaks of a place of safety, a refuge from enemies and the threatening powers around. The word com-fort, then, really means, with strength. The deeper meaning of the beatitude, then, is that the very ones who mourn, are fortified or made strong when they experience the blessing of God. They are not defeated or cast down. They are able to act with strength. The mystical touch of God supplies them with the strength they need. His strength comforts them. In other words, they can take any situation or condition that would make an average person mourn; and with God's blessing, they are changed so that instead of bitter tears and a life of mourning, they are made strong. They are comforted, and this in itself is the blessing Jesus offered. "Blessed are those who mourn for they shall be comforted."

You have known people like that. In the city of Calcutta, India, there is a school known as the Lee Memorial Mission. It could well be called the School of the Second Beatitude. The story behind this Mission School began in Darjeeling, a resort city, north of Calcutta, near the Tibetan border. At Darjeeling one looks out on the majestic Mount Kanchenjunga, the third highest peak in the world, and from near-by Tiger Hill one can catch glimpses of Mt. Everest on a clear day.

Early in this century, the Lees, a missionary family from America, were stationed in Calcutta. They sent their five children to the Mount Hermon School for missionary children in Darjeeling. Each summer the parents spent their holidays with their children, living in a home on the edge of a high mountain. On a certain week end, the parents were called back to Calcutta and the children were left in the care of the servants. Then the monsoon came. It rained and rained all week end. There may have been minor earthquakes as well. Sunday night the floods descended, washing mud and rock from the mountainside against the house; when morning came, both the house and that part of the mountain had vanished. Only one child had somehow managed to escape.

Word was immediately sent to the parents. They hurried back and searched but were unable to find any trace of the other four children. The Mission Board advised the Lees to take a furlough to recover from their loss, but the Lees responded, "Our family are now a part of the soil of India. We will stay here. We will not have five children, we will have five hundred. We will send word to Christians across the seas and they will help us build a school and provide scholarships in memory of our children."

31

That was what happened. I met Mrs. Lee when I visited the school in 1939 and whenever I went to Calcutta I stayed at the Lee Memorial Mission in Wellington Square. Year after year it has touched boys and girls with blessing—a blessing that came through the Lees who turned mourning into comfort.

It was at that Mission, too, that I met an Indian girl whose name is also Lee. Her father was head cook at the Mission and her brother, Emmanuel, came for a year's training in communications which I conducted, and stayed on to get special instruction under our electronics engineer. Eventually Emmanuel was employed by the Voice of America, but now helps a group make Christian radio programs in the Bengali language. The Indian girl was his sister. She was stricken with a crippling disease when she was a girl in school. She has been in her bed for more than forty years in a corner of the dormitory. Her bed is regularly surrounded by students, for in spite of her pain, there is always laughter and joy and the radiance of one who has received the blessing of God's comfort—strength to use her suffering to bring hope and Christian love to generation after generation of students.

The secret—not to give way to mourning or to be overcome with grief. That is not the blessing God offers us. God's blessing softens our grief as he makes us tender-hearted and prompts us to reach out to others helpfully, with strength. Comfort is expansive. Filling others with strength is a sure way to receive the blessing of comfort for ourselves. Jesus knew the full meaning of this in this own experience so he could put it into words that have meaning for all of us. "Blessed are those who mourn for they shall be comforted."

THE THIRST FOR RIGHTEOUSNESS

Matthew 5:6

"**B**lessed are those who hunger and thirst for righteousness, for they shall be satisfied."

In another meditation when we wrote of the beatitudes of Jesus, we noted that people of his day had almost a reverential attitude toward a blessing. God's blessing implied that something of the very righteous character of God rubbed off on those worthy of his blessing, and Jesus was saying that those who hungered and thirsted for righteousness would receive it in full. They would be satisfied. Nor could their quest for righteousness be satisfied apart from this special blessing of God. One was dependent on the other. Those who were unrighteous lacked much that made life worth while, which is another way of saying they forfeited God's blessing, so they were unsatisfied. But the righteous enjoyed full and completely satisfying lives.

You may ask, if a righteous life is so fulfilling, how can it be that so many professing Christians live colorless, unattractive, and anything but what one would call full and satisfying lives? There were religious people in Jesus' day who were stiff-necked, narrow-minded, self-righteous, prejudiced. In his revelation of God, those did not evidence the blessing he spoke of in this beatitude.

Jesus had a healthy view of what righteousness is. He saw many who stood on street corners and made long prayers to be seen of men. Some of them must have been narrow, mean, joyless, empty souls, for he said, all they wanted was to be seen of men but secretly they were full of dead men's bones. (Matthew 23:27) To Jesus, righteousness seemed to be whatever brought out the good, whatever made life better, whatever helped people live together in peace, whatever turned them from selfishness and made them concerned for their neighbors. The religion of Jesus was life-fulfilling. He cast aside all that hindered spiritual growth or blocked out truth. All claims of spiritual inspiration carry with them an overflowing sustaining righteousness. The injunction that we should love the Lord our God with our whole body, mind, soul, and strength, and our neighbor as ourselves, was the very essence of the "law and prophets." (Matthew 22:40) Here was satisfying righteousness.

Think for a minute how empty some lives are. Try to picture those whose lives center around things that cannot truly satisfy: lust, money, power, fame, thrills, lawlessness. They are not life-fulfilling. The more money one has the more he wants. The more power a Hitler has, the more he wants. The craze for fame or to be number one, or to get into a book of records, can become a sickness. One record demands another and then another. It is not satisfying or fulfilling. The poet was right, "A life without Christ is as empty as a last year's bird's nest."

Jesus was putting his finger on a central law of life; we are not meant to be happy when we are empty. This is written into the very fibers of our minds and bodies. When we are ignorant or dishonest or covetous, we are most miserable. Life is not satisfying when hate rules us, but we are joyously filled to overflowing when love controls us. Life is not satisfied when we are surrounded by filth, ugliness, and disharmony. We are delightfully satisfied with beauty, cleanliness, and harmony. Life is made for love, truth, beauty, righteousness. So Jesus was expressing a profound truth when he said, "Blessed are those who hunger and thirst for righteousness for they shall be satisfied."

We should note, further, that Jesus did not say, "Blessed are the righteous." He said, "Blessed are those who hunger and thirst for righteousness." He knew people who claimed to be righteous. They thought they had arrived. They were self-righteous and self-satisfied. They were static, spiritually dead. They had stopped growing, and they were not likable people. When we have an overwhelming spiritual experience, the danger is that we may assume that God has nothing more in store for us. That initial experience is so life-fulfilling. But no matter how great that early rapture, it is only a prelude to all God has in store for us. There is more. We must go on, as John Wesley said, to perfection or fulfillment. Going on is important. We are never to stop as long as we have breath. This hunger and thirst is a part of God's blessing. It sends us forward.

We get what we go after; or at least, we do not get what we do not go after. Righteousness doesn't just happen. Even as physical hunger and thirst compel us to provide food and drink for our bodies lest we die, so the soul's hunger and thirst calls for nourishment. To starve our souls is to dwarf and smother our potential. We miss the best life has to offer if we do not accept this blessing.

Possibly the reason there is so much evil in the world is that we who look upon ourselves as righteous people do not act with enough

34

dedication. Only when it is viewed as a matter of life and death with us can this blessing really be ours. If at any time our Christian experience seems empty or unsatisfying, it may be because we have ceased hungering and thirsting for what God wants to provide. But we can have the full and satisfying life Jesus offers in this beatitude if we go after it because we hunger and thirst for it. Only then will our lives be full and satisfying.

OTHER BEATITUDES

Matthew 5:7-9

The first three beatitudes directed our thoughts more to the individual. The next three speak more of our relations to others.

"Blessed are the merciful for they shall obtain mercy."

In giving this teaching, Jesus challenged his followers to make tenderness, love, and graciousness their way of life. Down through history, we Christians have so often done the opposite. Churchmen and groups of religious enthusiasts and so-called Christian rulers have at times forced their will on those they labeled heretics, or on persons of other religions, with a brutality and cruelty not found even among those they described as "heathen." Many evil things have been done "in the name of God." At times, one group of Christians showed no mercy to another group of Christians. Protestants rose up against Catholics; and Catholics, against Protestants. Both found excuses to dispossess the Jews and drive them from one land to another. Often the Mohammedans, who have often been regarded as cruel, were in fact more tolerant and more humane than the Christians. And nothing was more brutal than the wholesale destruction of the civilizations of Central and South American Indians. It was done in the name of the Church and sanctioned as a way to "Christianize" the land.

It has taken Christians a long time to learn the lessons of mercy. Violence is still the accepted form of conduct among many religious factions. The prolonged strife in Ireland, the atrocities and bloodshed in the Middle East, and injustices that lead to riots within our own nation often have strong religious sentiments supporting them. History tells us we have not yet learned to live in the spirit of this beautitude.

There was cruelty in Jesus' day. There were crosses on every highway, put there by the Roman rulers. Yet Jesus could say, "Blessed are the merciful for they shall obtain mercy." It was as if he were saying that those who are blessed of God must break the cycle of hate, revenge, and death. He threw out this challenge to his followers to start a crusade to break that cycle, to mercifully end the evils of revenge.

In the spiritual dawn of the Hebrews it was believed that God was a stern judge who would wipe out all the people of the earth by a flood, because they had sinned. Then the prophets discovered that God is a God of mercy and love and that his objective is not to destroy sinners or make them suffer, but to redeem sinners. Jesus based his beatitudes on that kind of a God. He spoke of God as a Good Shepherd who would lay down his life for his sheep. The Good Shepherd left the ninety and nine in search of one that was lost; when he found it, he came rejoicing. Our merciful God seeks out those who have sinned and are lost. "While we were yet sinners, Christ died for us." (Romans 5:8) Even as God is merciful, we should be merciful, even to our enemies, and find ways to appeal to the good in them for their and our good. We must learn this finer way to deal with evil in the world. Abraham Lincoln learned it. "The way to destroy an enemy is to make him your friend."

This beatitude is a powerful new concept. Jesus saw that acting unmercifully started a chain reaction of atrocity, cruel exploitation, evil, and death. But acting mercifully also starts a chain reaction that is positive and leads to justice, mutual prosperity, civilized development. The one arises out of cowardice, fear, and prejudice. The other exhibits courage, faith, and mutual understanding. A weakling is often unmerciful. It takes a person who is strong and outgoing to show mercy. Jesus was not willing to settle for anything less than one's full potential. God's blessing falls not only on the one who shows mercy but on him on whom mercy is shown. "Blessed are the merciful for they shall obtain mercy."

"Blessed are the pure in heart for they shall see God."

A man complained to his neighbor that his eyesight was growing dim. When he looked out his windows he saw gray and fuzzy things. The neighbor came in, washed his windows and to the man's amazement, he could see things as clearly and as beautifully as ever.

Many of us allow the windows of our souls to become unclean. An experience comes that shakes our faith. Doubts arise, fears take over. Anxieties overwhelm us. We even fail to thank God for the food we eat or the beauty of a rose or the kindness of a friend. The windows of our souls get clouded over. Life loses its purity and goodness through cloudy windows.

It takes a brave soul and a soul that has deep spiritual roots to keep his windows clean. We must be pure in heart; then we begin to discover that God is in his world and we are able to see God all about us. God is in nature. The poet said that if he could understand what makes a rose so beautiful, he could explain the other secrets of life. The pure in heart can see God at his work of redemption—his caring for the suffering and the weak. What if those who are most desperate and hopeless in the world had no God to turn to; they could not endure. He is their strengh, their only comfort, their only hope. Such peace, joy, and hope come only to the pure in Heart. When their eyes are opened to the presence of God, when they are aware that he is at work in the world around them, they are truly blessed. To see God because their hearts are pure, is indeed a blessing.

*"Blessed are the peacemakers for they shall be called
the sons of God."*

One of the Chinese words for peace includes two signs: the sign for heart and beside it two parallel lines. When two hearts are parallel or equal there is peace. When one heart tries to gain advantage over the other, there is conflict. Peace is when two people are in right relationship with each other. Peacemakers' hearts lie parallel and stay that way. The night Jesus came to earth there were songs, "Peace on earth, goodwill toward men." It was as if God were saying, "Here is my Son—to live and work among you so that your heart and my heart may be parallel. You may know peace because there is a right relationship between us forevermore." A peace built on such a relationship is the only true basis for peace between individuals and nations. When we know this peace, we begin acting like the sons of God. This doesn't come in our own strength but only when we receive God's blessing. It takes sons of God to know peace.

We recall how at the end of the first World War the Allies tried to crush Germany and put economic demands on her that made her go bankrupt. It was not a peace of reconciliation or redemption. It was a peace of revenge. The lines between the nations did not lie parallel but they crossed each other to inflict punishment, no doubt where some punishment was due, but when it was accompanied by vengeance it was self-destructive. This led to the second World War. After that war, because we had learned our lesson, we offered the Marshall Plan so that the conquered and the conquerors might live parallel, as equals, and so that, in time, our hearts might beat together as one again. What a difference that has made.

Lasting peace, either within our minds and hearts, or between people and nations, comes as a blessing when we determine in our hearts to act like "sons of God." Jesus said, "You are to be makers of peace because your hearts are right, because you are the sons of God." When we let the blessing of God flow through us and we act in ways parallel to the love of God we become the peacemakers of the world.

TAKE MY YOKE

Matthew 11:28-30

What may seem impossible to us one moment may be accomplished with relative ease at another time. This ability to release our energies in this manner remains somewhat a mystery, but there are helpful hints if we look for them. The Christian home in which I grew up contributed much to my understanding of the way life works.

My father was a dedicated Christian minister. He had a poem for every occasion and a vivid story for many. He once told of an old teacher who took a group of eager children on an outing. You know how hard it is to keep children from running and jumping until they are ready to drop. Some child would shout, "See what I found," and everyone would run to see, then they would race here and there, and of course there were always trees to climb.

When it came time to start home someone asked, "How far is it?" When the teacher said, "Two miles," there was a chorus of groans and one little boy's lips began to quiver as tears came to his eyes and he said, "I am so tired. I can't go another step," and before the teacher could think of anything to say or do, there were half a dozen who began to howl. Others sat down and moaned and groaned.

Two miles! Well, the teacher might carry one, but he couldn't carry twenty. Suddenly he had an idea. He went across the road and began cutting some canes that grew there. Some of the children howled all the louder because they thought he was getting switches to use on them, but he wasn't. Back he came with an armload of canes and said, "You won't have to walk home. See, I've found some horses. You can ride." And putting the largest cane between his legs he pretended he was riding a prancing horse.

After a minute there was a scramble for canes. Everyone took one, and off they went—racing and prancing and all excited with the new game. Where did their crying go? I thought they were so tired they couldn't take another step. Something had triggered new energy. Someone had lifted the burden, and instead of exhaustion there was energy to spare and joy in every moment of it.

People had a way of coming to Jesus carrying their heavy burdens of sin or guilt or anger, or just being worn out. He welcomed them and on one very special day, said, "Come unto me, all who labor and are heavy laden, and I will give you rest. Take my yoke upon you and learn from me, for I am gentle and lowly in heart, and you will find rest for your souls. For my yoke is easy, and my burden is light."

The yoke he offered was like the canes the teacher gave the children. You may never have seen a yoke. I've seen thousands of them on the bullocks who draw carts in India. The yoke serves much like a horse collar—put a bad collar on a horse and soon he has a sore neck and is unable to work. Put on a good collar and he can put his full strength against any load.

Jesus said, "Take my yoke." Most yokes are double. Two animals pull together. Jesus was saying, "Be yoked to me. There isn't any load we can't pull together."

One night in India, when I was on a railway train, a soldier, who had been drinking, stretched out on the place assigned to me and left me standing without a place to sit down. There were fifteen or twenty other soldiers in the large compartment and a number of civilians, all of whom saw what had happened. As I looked around, I realized they were watching to see what I would do. Somehow I did not get angry. I felt suddenly the need for strength and courage; it seemed in a very real way there was a restraining hand that helped me act far better than I could without the spiritual help that came right then. I was yoked to greater understanding and wisdom than I myself had and I was very much aware of it.

Things happened very quickly. The train had just started from the station, so, to stop it, another soldier reached up and pulled the emergency cord. Even before the train stopped other soldiers came and lifted the drunken soldier from my reserved area. They held him for the military police who came to find out what was wrong. They were going to take him off the train but I asked them to leave him, saying that I was sure he would not molest me any more. I suddenly realized I was among friends. Soon we were on our way again, but the moment stands out clear and memorable. It was one of those rare moments that can come to any of us when some divine power steps in to turn what could be a catastrophy into a peaceful ending. I knew without doubt I was yoked to a power greater than myself and it transformed my responses and gave me understanding that was so greatly needed just then.

What I really want to say is this. You will have moments when you feel like crying, like those children, or you are so tired and discouraged or lonely that you cannot go on. Then it is you need the yoke Jesus offers you. You don't have to pull this burden alone. You can be yoked to him. In your hearts say, "Jesus, you have promised to help. I want that help now. There isn't anything I can't handle as long as I am yoked to Jesus."

THE GOOD THAT IS IN US

II Corinthians 4:1-12, Genesis 1, 2:7

"We have this treasure in earthen vessels, to show that the good that is in us (the transcendent power) belongs to God and not to us."

One of the amazing thoughts found in the Bible is the story of man's creation. We are told that God took the dust of the earth and shaped it into a man and breathed into him the breath of life, and man became a living soul. (Genesis 1)

It was always fascinating to watch a country potter at work in India. He had what looked almost like a wagon wheel lying just above the level of the ground. It was fitted onto an axle, sometimes a perfectly shaped rock that permitted the wheel to turn with a minimum of friction. He mixed the dust of the ground with water and when it was just the right consistency, he took a lump of it and put it at the center of the wheel. He then stood and fitted a stick into a hole in the rim of the wheel; with that he started the wheel spinning until it was moving at tremendous speed. As he squatted down over the wheel his skilled hands touched the clay, shaping it into an earthen vessel, so perfectly, so graceful, so amazing. Then, taking a razor thin piece of bamboo, he sliced under the clay pot, at precisely the right spot, cutting the bottom of the vessel from the spinning wheel, and with a skill that he had gained through experience, he lifted the vessel from the still spinning wheel and set it on the ground to dry.

Clay pots and vessels have been made from almost the dawn of history. The march of civilization can be traced by examining the pottery found at different levels of a culture. I picked up a shard or a piece of pottery from the ruins of the palace of Nebuchadnezzar, near Bagdad in Iraq; I treasure it greatly. It tells me something about people who lived long ago.

Paul reminds us that we are only clay vessels that contain a great treasure. "We have this treasure in earthen vessels, to show that the good that is in us belongs to God."

We are all clay vessels. The greatest men and women differ from others, not because they are not of clay so much as because of the treasure they have in them. Every great person has feet of clay. Read your history. George Washington was an amazing man—the father of our country—who lived through Valley Forge and defeated the armies that were sent against him by the most powerful nation of his day. But you will read pages of criticism of Washington written by his contemporaries who looked on his early failures with complaining eyes. What was true of Washington, was also true of Lincoln. Once during a period of biting criticism he declared that he was doing the best he could and would do it to the end. "If the end brings me out all right," he added, "what is said against me won't amount to anything. If the end brings me out wrong, ten angels swearing I was right would make no difference." Every President has feet of clay, and each has been reminded of it many times a day.

You and I know we are fragile earthen vessels. Yesterday I said something to a friend and afterwards I realized he might misunderstand and it would hurt him. There was no way of taking it back, but I realized what I said was very unkind. When we do things that hurt others we realize we have feet of clay.

41

But we need not stop there. God has breathed into this clay of ours a breath of life and we become living souls. We are endowed with the power to respond to God and he will fill our hearts with a power for good, even though we are vessels of clay. All this we find in a man known as Augustine—a frail weak vessel who in his youth lived such a corrupt life it almost broke the heart of his mother, Monica. But the day came when Augustine felt God's love overpower him and Augustine, the sinner, became Saint Augustine, the Bishop of Hippo. God's treasure was released in that vessel of clay, and he gave utterance to words that have stirred every generation since, "Our souls are restless until they find their rest in thee." He appeared on the horizon of history at that moment when Christianity was at its crossroads, struggling to lift civilization above the decaying Roman Empire. So great was this treasure in him that he put new life into the Christian movement throughout the then known world.

We find another such man much closer to our own time. There were few in England in the eighteenth century who would not agree that a certain John Bunyan was a man of clay. Like so many of his century he was barely literate. He was thrown into Bedford jail because he could not pay his debts and there he languished for many years—yet he did not languish, for while in jail he unearthed a treasure. He discovered that the good in us belongs to God and that it is for man to release it. He put this in a book, *Pilgrim's Progress*, which many were later to say was the greatest book of his century. It has circled the globe in one translation after another. What a magnificent treasure John Bunyan had in his vessel of clay.

When you hold a mirror and see your image in it, the reflection is of an "earthen vessel," but looking closer you find that the vessel embodies a soul. There is a glow in your eyes, a spiritual vitality in your visage, a love showing in the lines of your face, a stirring to let loose the power of God, not only in your life but among those with whom you live. Yes, we need to remind ourselves, we carry these wonderful gifts of God in earthen vessels: weak, sinful, fragile, but they can be stamped with the image of God and we become of infinite worth. The value of the treasure in us is measured by how fully and perfectly we have permitted the Potter to give shape and meaning to our lives.

MAKE TODAY COUNT

Psalm 90:1-4, 10, 12, 16, 17

When I read the story of Orville Kelley of Burlington, Iowa, I was so impressed, I decided I must share what I came to know about him. It was not what happened to him that was so unusual, but the way he handled it. Fortunately, when he was told he had cancer, a disease that touches an increasing number in our society, he was also told that it is a myth that all who have the disease have only a short time to live. Some are cured by treatment and many others who cannot be cured, suffer either little or no pain. Because of Kelley's courageous handling of his disease, he has been an inspiration to thousands who suffer in a similar way.

Though Orville Kelley is an extraordinary man, his immediate reaction, on learning he had the disease, was quite normal. He went into a tail-spin emotionally. He sulked and felt sorry for himself, and was so overcome that he wanted to hide himself; he carried this to the extent he almost stopped communicating with his wife. He did not want his children to be informed, but they clearly saw something was wrong and went through a period when they were terribly confused. It was only after he began chemotherapy treatments at the University of Iowa Hospitals and Clinics in 1973 that he began to understand the disease and his attitude began to change.

No one knows exactly what brought about that change. For many, cancer seems to spell out the word death, and Kelley did not want to die. He dreaded the thought that his children would have to grow up without him, and that he no longer would share in Christmas and other family festivals. He was filled with fear. Then he began to get ahold of himself. He explains it this way. "I stopped allowing my fright to consume my days and nights." Part of his recovery was due to his discovery that "people who have been tapped on the shoulder by death seem to live a more complete life in the time they have left. They lead pretty normal lives under abnormal circumstances." This turn-about in his mental attitude contributed much to what doctors look upon as added years to his life.

As he probed for what had led to this discovery he noted that soon after his treatments began he came to realize "that the emotional and psychological problems associated with his condition were more devastating than the illness itself." Then he thought, if this were true for him, it was probably true for others. He began to formulate ways he could share this discovery so that others who suffer from the same disease might have this information and it would help them overcome their fears.

His earlier experience as a newspaper editor and reporter now proved tremendously helpful. He wrote an article for a local paper telling what it was like to live with cancer, and he told much he had learned out of his own experience. He was almost overwhelmed when his article brought a flood of mail and phone calls. It was clear there were many all across the country who wanted to help each other cope with their disease, and he decided he wanted to help them pool their experiences. So in January, 1974, eighteen of them met at the Burlington Elks Club and out of that meeting, a self-help organization, *Make Today Count*, was formed. During the five years following, more than 200 chapters were organized in the United States, Canada, and Australia.

This seemed to turn Kelley around. He stopped feeling sorry for himself and found new strength. He informed his friends, "I do not consider myself dying of cancer, but rather living despite of it. I no longer think of each passing day as another day closer to death, but rather as another day of life."

This vital change became his "gospel of hope," and he began to barnstorm the country, visiting hospitals and going into private homes to see patients. He maintained that along with physical treatments there is another, "tender loving care," and "what cancer victims look for is someone to reach out, hold their hands, squeeze their arms. Someone who'll look them in the eye. Someone who cares." When they find a physician who does this, his "friendship and caring is more important to the patient than medical expertise."

There is much more we could tell about Orville Kelley. What I have written was reported in the "Parade Magazine" in 1980 in an article by the journalist, Howard L. Rosenberg. The article went on to say that Kelley may have been a victim of occupational exposure. For a time he had been with a squad of men, sent by the government, to test atomic bombs in the Pacific. Exposure to radiation at that time may have led to his cancer. He believed so and this belief spurred him to rally his energies in an effort to persuade the Government to provide treatment for all those who had been exposed. It took him to Washington and elsewhere in his effort to help others.

The story of a courageous man like Orville Kelley is an inspiration to all of us. It was only after he accepted his disease and permitted others to help him that changes in both his mind and body began. Later, when he discovered that he could help others face their disease and began reaching out to touch others, the most remarkable changes took place. He learned how terribly important compassion and tender love was for his own well-being and what it could do for others. At no time could anyone assure Kelley he would be cured, nor could he give such assurance to others, but when he and they began to accept each day, not as a day closer to death, but as another day of life, they experienced profound changes in their personalities. They learned to make today count.

Every day is really a precious gift to each one of us. I was never more aware of this than during the second World War. For days and weeks I was in convoy crossing the south Atlantic and going up the east coast of Africa. Our ships seemed barely to move over an endless sea. Often to escape the heat of my cabin in the depths of the ship, I would stretch out at night on the hard deck and try to sleep. Then as I awoke in the morning and saw the sun break out of the vast ocean, a hymn just naturally came to mind out of gratitude for another day and I would sing, "When morning guilds the sky, my soul awakening cries, may Jesus Christ be praised."

You and I have been given another day. We need to fill it to the full. Like Orville Kelley we can live only one day at a time but it will mean more if we remember his motto, *Make Today Count.* Right now we can know something of the joy and happiness that helped Orville Kelley, a man with cancer, find such a good and full life.

DISCOVERING LIFE'S TREASURES

John 4:3-15

A song that fired the imagination of youth of the past generation speaks of "the impossible dream." It seems to be in our blood to respond to what some say is impossible. And a secret of successful living is to attach ourselves to what is greater and better than ourselves. It seems to draw out the best that is in us. Mothers dream dreams for their children. Children build aircastles. And until something grips a person and fires his imagination, he is likely just to drift. It takes something of the spirit of a dreamer to discover life's treasures.

Of course a person could waste his whole life chasing idle dreams. Ponce de Leon tramped the Florida marshes battling hostile Indians who killed off scores of his soldiers—and what was he after? He dreamed there was a fountain of perpetual youth, and he wasted his and many other lives trying to find it.

Or there was Ali Hafed, a Persian, made famous by Dr. Russel R. Conwell in his famous lecture, "Acres of Diamonds." Ali was a prosperous, happy farmer-businessman who lived along the Indus River in India. One day a Buddhist priest came by and told him of diamonds, those priceless gems that were so valuable that if one possessed even a few he could put his children on the thrones of great countries and he would be the happiest man in the world. Ali began to dream.

He sold all he possessed and after providing for his family, he set out to find diamonds. The Buddhist monk had told him he would find them in white sand in a crystal clear stream flowing between high mountains. Ali travelled from country to country, hunting down every possible clue, until at last he stood on the shores at Barcelona. He was in rags. His money was gone and he had not found the white sands nor the diamonds. In despair when a tidal wave swept in through the pillars of Hercules, Ali cast himself into the incoming waves and was drowned.

Some months later, the Buddhist priest returned to the same farm where Ali had lived. The man who bought it, when he was near the clear stream that flowed over white sand in Ali's fields, caught sight of a black stone that had what looked like a window of light in it. When he looked closer he noted that it reflected all the colors of the rainbow, so he took it home and put it on the mantle. That was where the Priest found it and asked where it had come from. The new owner told him and together they went to the stream and discovered other diamonds, for that was what it was. Here were diamonds of untold value in the very stream that Ali had sold.

The story teller goes on to say that this farm became the famous Golconda diamond mines in which the Kohinoor and the Orloff diamonds of the crown jewels of England and Russia, were found. Ali's treasure had not been in some distant country but right at home all the time. Part of the "impossible dream" is to learn this truth— that often life's greatest treasure is right under our feet—within our grasp—most often right within ourselves.

Jesus was one who took this urge—this power to dream—and transferred it to the spiritual realm. To the young men who grouped around him he painted the dream of the Kingdom of God or the Kingdom of Heaven. This kingdom was not so much a place, for Jesus said it was within them. It was in the white sands of their souls. They had been catching fish, now they would be fishers of men. They would give up life on a low level, and they would find it on a higher. They would release the treasures of their souls.

Jesus had a way of starting people to look for this impossible dream—this inner treasure within them. He met the woman of Samaria at Jacob's well. There was a tension between them, for the writer comments that the woman didn't expect Jesus to speak to her because Jews had no dealings with Samaritans—there were prejudices way back then. But Jesus did ask her to give him water from the well and after she expressed surprise, Jesus went on to say, "If you knew the gift of God, and who it is that is saying to you 'Give me a drink,' you would have asked him and he would have given you living water. ... Everyone who drinks of this water (from Jacob's well) will thirst again, but whoever drinks of the water that I shall give him will never thirst; the water that I shall give him will become in him a spring of water welling up to eternal life."

She was a true Ponce de Leon. She completely missed what Jesus was saying. She wanted a perpetually filled water-jar. "Sir, give me this water, that I may not thirst, nor come here to draw." What Jesus wanted was not to give her a drink but to release rivers of water— hidden treasures of her life—rivers that would not dry up but run eternally. There were acres of diamonds in the white sands of her soul that she had lived with all her life but had never discovered and

Jesus said, "Discover those hidden treasures. Turn loose those rivers of living water."

We wonder why this woman did not accept the water of life Jesus offered or why Ali failed to discover diamonds on his farm but at last died on a distant shore. Yet, how many of the hidden treasures in the white sands of our souls have we discovered? As someone has said, "The only way to make a dream come true is to wake up." Jesus offers us the greatest treasures of life. "The water that I shall give will become in him a well of water welling up to eternal life." We need to wake up and discover God's treasure in the white sands of our souls.

TEMPTATION

Matthew 4:1-11; Colossians 1:1-14

This meditation was first used among those who resided in a skilled nursing facility. I include it here because there may come a time when a number of those who read these pages will find themselves living in a more restricted environment, and that calls for mental and spiritual preparation. I have discovered that even within those narrower boundaries, a person's spirit and compassion may remain free and that the essential issues of life can be handled courageously and helpfully with God's help, in fact those who do not avail themselves of his help are often crushed under the pressures of trying to live in their own strength.

My readers will be somewhat surprised when they see the subject I have chosen. It all goes to show that as long as we have breath we have much the same spiritual needs, wherever we live, so the intent of this meditation is to relate God's blessing to everyone who will open his or her life to God.

You may ask, "Who is tempted here? We cannot get out and rob a bank. We have to obey fixed rules within this nursing facility. Who is tempted?"

It just happens that all of us face temptations every day, even every hour. You may be tempted to be cross with a nurse who is a bit late or tempted to say a harsh word to a person in your room. You may feel

48

especially miserable, so you are tempted not to put forth the extra effort to look nice or be kind and cheerful. You see, there are many ways you can be tempted. When you are, here are some things to remember.

Temptations come to everyone. You wouldn't think that Jesus would be tempted, but he was. A person could hardly face more decisive temptations than Jesus did, as we are told in the Gospel of Matthew. We are told that he was tempted at every point just as we are, but he met his temptations head-on, and was without sin. He found he must turn to God for help, just as we do.

How we respond to temptations depends on the kind of persons we are. There is good and bad in all of us; and so, without outside help, sometimes we are good and sometimes we are bad. A poem by Ella Wheeler Wilcox tells us an important truth.

> One ship drives east and another drives west
> with the selfsame winds that blow;
> 'Tis the set of the sails and not the gales
> which tell us the way to go.
> Like the winds of the sea are the ways of fate,
> as we journey along through life;
> 'Tis the set of the soul that decides the goal,
> and not the calm or the strife.

The set of the soul! Much the same winds blow on all of us and we are all tempted. The wind doesn't determine how we will act. Outside pressures do not dictate our responses. It is the set of the sail, the set of the soul that decides the goal. If we are persons guided by an inner strength, we will steer our course straight no matter whether in calm or strife. We need those inner controls. They are our sure defense against yielding to evil temptations.

When we look for the source of inner strength in Jesus we see that he was constantly drawing power from God. We read how Jesus went from his disciples from time to time, to a mountain top, or out into the desert, or into a boat, then later into the Garden of Gethsemane, to pray. There he set the course of his life—"Not my will but thine be done." He used lines of communication with God; and when he was tempted he made use of those lines and God's power flowed into him. Archbishop Trench tells how that inner strength can be ours.

Lord, what a change within us one short hour
Spent in Thy presence will avail to make!
What heavy burdens from our bosom take;
What parched ground refresh, as with a shower.
We kneel, and all around us seems to lower;
We rise, and all the distant and the near
Stands forth in sunny outline, brave and clear.
We kneel how weak! We rise how full of power!
Why therefore, should we do ourselves this wrong,
Or others, that we are not always strong;
That we should ever weak or heartless be,
Anxious or troubled, when with us is prayer
And joy and strength and courage are with Thee?

It is when we are weak spiritually we yield to temptation and sometimes we excuse ourselves saying, "The devil tempted me, so I yielded." In talking with a resident in the Shores, some time ago, he said, "Yes, the devil can tempt a person; but when we yield to the devil it is because we want to." He went on, "It is not the devil who is strong, for God has the final word. If we really want to obey God, then the devil cannot control us."

St. Paul confirms this in a verse he has written in his letter to the Colossians. (1:13) "He (God) has delivered us from the dominion of darkness (the power of the devil) and transferred us to the kingdom of his beloved Son, in whom we have redemption, the forgiveness of sins." When we take hold of the power God offers us, we can face up to any temptation and meet it triumphantly.

You are people who face temptation every day. I think it takes more outgoing love and kindness, more strength of character, more dependence on inner strength to live in a health care center week after week than almost any other place. With the help of God you can do it graciously and with strength, for you can have the help of God to meet temptations as they come. That help is yours now, for the asking.

THE WAY OF LOVE WORKS

Hosea 2, 3, 11:8f.

There is a tombstone in one of the military cemetaries in Jabalpur, India, that apparently summed up the life of what must have been a pretty shady character, "The wages of sin is death."

That pronouncement is pretty much a traditional observation that fails to take into account God's full plan for the redemption of mankind. True, throughout the early history of the Hebrews, when their spiritual understanding was primitive, they believed that the usual way God dealt with sinners was to destroy them. This is found in numerous stories of the Bible. But in the spiritual upreach of those remarkable people, there finally broke on their slow and dull minds the understanding that God's real purpose was not to destroy but redeem the wicked. God agonized over them as he tried to draw his people from their evil so they would learn of him and give themselves to righteousness. He longed for their redemption, for he knew that only as they turned to him could they begin to live up to their high potential.

It is very probable that we can open the pages of history and observe when this enlarged spiritual understanding was first revealed to man. The prophet Hosea made this discovery.

Hosea learned that God is a God of love through a tragic domestic experience. Gomer, his wife, was unfaithful. She had sunk lower and lower into sin until she had become not only a common prostitute but her sale price was exceedingly low. She could not go much lower. This was repulsive to Hosea as he reflected with agonizing pain the effect of her sin upon their children. Had he acted as husbands usually did, he would have denounced her and left her in her degradation, but he could not. He was amazed to find a deepening love within his heart that compelled him to try to win her back. This was not a passionate feeling, but he was moved with compassion because of what was happening to her. So he went down to the marketplace and bought her back from her lovers, though he did not fully understand at first why he did it.

Giving the matter further thought Hosea realized that his response was above and beyond the tenderness he, an ordinary mortal, had ever experienced. This had come as he listened to God. He concluded that God was reaching through this human experience

51

to reveal to him a new understanding about the very nature of God. He came to see that he had acted as he had, because God had put it in his heart to do so; God had put it in his heart, because that was what was in the heart of God. From this Hosea concluded, God is a God of love and longs not for the punishment of sinners but for their redemption. He saw this as a higher law—a spiritual law that had profound implications.

In that early day it was an amazing discovery, one that Ezekiel and later Jesus were to apply to all of life. Hosea extended his discovery to reinterpret God's attitude toward his nation, Israel. He admitted that his nation deserved to be punished, because they had turned from the worship of Jehovah, their God, to worship Baal, the Canaanite god. God's words through Hosea to the nation were almost the same as the word that had come to Hosea about Gomer. "How can I give you up, O Ephraim? (Ephraim was a familiar name for Israel) How can I hand you over, O Israel?. . . . My compassion grows warm and tender. I will not execute my fierce anger. I will not again destroy Ephraim; for I am God and not man, the Holy One in your midst, and I will not come to destroy." (Hosea 11:8f.)

In many ways we are a hard-hearted people. So many of us still doubt whether the way of love works. Our criminal procedures are directed to the punishment of wrongdoers rather than loving them back into society. Love is more costly in time and money than simply locking a person up; it takes longer and calls for more patience to redeem a sinner. Probably most of our failures can be attributed to our lack of love and compassion. We are still waiting for a breakthrough in the process of redemption. Surely God's way is our only hope. I was all the more convinced of this when I heard the story of Aunt Hannah, as Dr. William Stidger told it. It points up a need to release God's love in a finer way in our lives.

The setting of Aunt Hannah's story is Baltimore. Some years ago a professor in John Hopkins University sent his students into a poor section of the city to find whether there was any link between poverty and crime. Their findings were recorded on a set of 200 cards. The cards were put in a file with the notation, "Headed for Crime." Then the cards were forgotten. Some years later, another professor found the cards and assigned his students the task of hunting up the persons earlier interviewed. The students naturally went first to police records, but to their amazement they found only two out of the 200 who had criminal records. What had happened?

That was where Aunt Hannah came in. She had taught in the grades for forty years. Aunt Hannah's name appeared on the records of person after person. When they interviewed a man whose card had the heading, "Headed for jail," he admitted, "I was headed for jail all right, until Aunt Hannah got hold of me and started me in the right direction." One doctor reported, "I was really a bad egg; so bad that the police pinned every crime in the neighborhood on me, and often they were right." Then one day Aunt Hannah told him to stay after school. "She didn't scold me, she didn't threaten me. She talked to me with a mother's love. I had no mother and had never known such love. Then she said, 'Come, have Sunday dinner with me.' I went, and somehow after that I simply couldn't let Aunt Hannah down."

The students found others. One was the owner of a large grocery store. His story was much the same. He admitted that as a boy, working in the store, he would steal candy and groceries and sometimes money. Finally he was caught. His employer was going to send him to jail. Then the boy went to Aunt Hannah. Two days later she kept him after school. "You won't have to go to jail," she said, "but you will have to pay back everything you have stolen." He was proud to add, "I was even able to keep my job, and I paid it all back and kept on until I was able to buy the store. Her love kept me out of jail."

Others told much the same story; and from the reports received, Dr. Stidger reminds us, "He who does not love his brother whom he has seen, cannot love God whom he has not seen. . . . for God is love." (I John 4:20) Jesus gave a deeper spiritual insight to what Hosea had discovered centuries before.

Thank God for the Aunt Hannahs who have touched our lives. Thank God for Hosea and the band of the faithful who have come after him who have helped open up our understanding of God's love. Nothing in all the world is as redemptive as love. Hosea discovered it, Jesus demonstrated it, and we can experience it. Love puts demands on us that seem to arouse our potential, opening to us spiritual experiences that are the highest and best life has to offer.

TRUE HAPPINESS

John 15:1-17

There are times the average person feels very much alone. Though we are surrounded by friends and relatives and take part in activities such as games, parties, and a worship service, still there are moments of loneliness. That was true when I travelled extensively. How often I would go into a great hotel swarming with people. Rooms were filled. Crowds were on the streets outside, but when I shut my door and shut out the sounds, so often I felt cut off— very much alone. This experience can come to us at times, no matter where we are.

There are ways to overcome loneliness. Jesus pointed out that we can establish a deep and stimulating spiritual relationship with God that does not permit us to feel alone. He compared that relationship to a vine and its branches. In the scripture reading we find this very helpful picture of the life of one who believes in God. If I understand him correctly, I believe Jesus was saying something like this:

"I am the vine, you are the branches." Then he added, "No branch can bear fruit if it is cut off from the vine, for the vine is its source of life. A branch, cut off, soon withers and dries up. Now," he said, "since I am the vine and you are the branches, food and strength flows from me so you can bear much fruit. You are fully alive. Those who cut themselves off from me and rely on the branch itself for food, wither spiritually and die. They become discouraged and helpless. They are weak and defeated. They can do nothing."

He added, "If you abide in me. ..." We often pass over the word "abide" without thinking what it means as it is used here. To abide is a continuing situation, a sustaining relationship, such as is found between a vine and its branches so the juices of life—food, water, chemicals—flow day after day from the vine into the branch. "If you abide, if you have that sustaining relationship, and my words abide in you so that they constantly feed and sustain you; there is no end to what you can do. You can put demands on yourself and you will have the strength to carry them out, 'you can ask whatever you will, and it shall be done for you.'"

That is what life is all about. We glorify and please God, not when we are weak or cut off from him, but when we draw strength from the vine to bear much fruit—to live a vigorous and good life. That is

54

what spiritual fellowship means. That is what discipleship is—when we get strength from God through Jesus Christ.

Jesus went on to say that we should never feel alone for no one ever needs to feel cut off from God's love. Because of that love, God sent Jesus to show what he is like. Jesus knew the love of God fully, and he could think of nothing that would be of greater good for us than that we might know his Father as a God of love. He went on to say, "If you ever feel alone, remember you are not cut off. All the love that God has given me I am pushing out through the vine into the branches. 'As my father has loved me, even so I have loved you, for we are vine and branch together.'"

Again he used the word "abide." "Abide in that love." Feel it every moment of every day. Feel it when you are lonely. Feel it when you are discouraged. Let that love lift you out of your heartache and pain. Surely he was saying, "Let it fill your whole life, day by day, every moment, especially when you begin to feel alone. You never need be alone for you can have his love flowing into you every moment."

It might seem that when Jesus says that the branch must bear fruit, he is putting heavy demands on us. What he is really pointing out is that this is what follows naturally—this is what actually happens in fulfillment of God's law of love and life. We become fruit bearers. Rather than withdraw from life and hide that love, rather than fail to bear fruit, we are enabled by his love to bear fruit. Fruit bearing is obedience to the law of love, so he says, "keep my commandments." It is permitting that obedience Jesus showed his Father to flow from the vine into the branches. We are acting from the same source of strength—the same life principal as Jesus—for he is the vine and we are the branches, so we are able to perfectly fulfill the commandments.

All this may seem complicated. We wonder how it can possibly be. Jesus goes on to say, "Rejoice—cheer up—these things have I spoken to you that my joy may be in you and that your joy may be full."

So in truth, we never need to be lonely again. We may become branches attached to the true vine. The vine is full of life, and it lets the love of God flow unhindered into every branch until each one of us can bear much fruit. This is the joy Jesus talks about, a joy that comes as we experience the abiding love of God in our lives and as we pass his love on as good fruit to others.

Yes, true religion should bring us this joy. It should add joy and laughter and delight to our lives. We are not alone in the world. We are branches attached to the true vine which is the source of every abiding good that can come to us.

A LOOK AT OURSELVES

Luke 15:11-24

We are familiar with the story of the Prodigal Son. There are many wonderful truths found in the story but I want to focus on only one of them. Here was a boy who left home and family and sowed his wild oats; and like others, he found that sinning wasn't all it was claimed to be. It dragged him lower and lower in human misery until he not only lost all that his father had given him of his wealth, but he lost about all of his self-respect. We are told he was about to starve and "fain would fill his belly with the husks intended for the swine," but even these were denied him, for about the time he began to feed on the husks, apparently the master appeared and knocked him to the ground. As he was lying there, he began to think of what he might have been. Even the servants in his father's house had enough to eat and clothing to wear, and here he was destitute and about to starve. The scripture tells us, "He came to himself," and said, "I will arise and go to my father, and will say, I am unworthy. ..."

His whole life story turned on that moment when he came to himself and said, "I will arise." Like the prodigal, many a person has gotten himself into a desperate situation before he faces up to what he has allowed to happen to him. Some have glorified ideas of themselves and are brought face to face with what they are. Others have lost their self-respect, not necessarily because they have indulged in a sinful life, but because of changes that have brought their spirits low. They need to come to themselves and take a fresh look at their lives.

We who are aging probably belong among those who have experienced many changes. Our tendency is to remember what we used to be and what we used to do and how we could get about and do things easily. Some may even have been the life of the party. Now that world has crumbled, and we feel almost as bad as that young boy did.

56

Those friends best able to help us remind us that we need to "come to ourselves." We must see ourselves as we are now. And when we take a fresh look, we begin to see that there is a glory and a meaning to life at each age of our existence. The things we are able to do now may be different. We can actually do some things better. My father used to say, "I cannot do everything. I will not let what I cannot do keep me from doing what I can." It pays to take an honest look at one's self.

An unthinking youth spoke out when he saw an older person who was struggling to walk, and said, "I never want to get old." Well, he doesn't have to. He may die young. But how fortunate we are to be among the living. We need to "come to ourselves," and take a fresh look.

What do we discover? Growing old is part of living. We should be proud of our age. Society is gaining respect for older people who do. Increasingly there are more activities and organizations that focus on the dignity and worth of those who are older. Institutional care of the elderly is now evaluated by its faithfulness to enhance human values and help people live up to their full potential, whatever their age.

When we come to ourselves we ask, how can I make these years before me meaningful and worthy? I must arise and face them and use all the resources God has given me so that I can keep alert and cheerful. I must exercise both body and mind and live to the full within my environment.

Our canes, our wheelchairs, our walkers become a part of us. We can laugh a little at ourselves, but how wonderful some of these aids are: glasses, false teeth, hearing aids, chemicals that relieve some of our aches and pains. We shouldn't imagine that we are the only ones who use such things. Recently in my reading I ran across a paragraph from a play written 300 years ago that described a young woman who was then acting on the stage in London. It says, "Her teeth were made in Blackfriars (a section of the city), her eyebrows in the Strand (another area), and her hair on Silver street. She takes herself asunder, when she goes to bed, into some 20 boxes, and about noon the next day is put together again like a German clock."

When we come to ourselves we see that we are older. But we see much more. We see that we are comforted and supported in cleanliness and health and good nursing. Nearby are those who are ready to add new experiences to our lives. How really fortunate we are. We can thank God for things to do with our hands, for those in the community who volunteer to help us, for those who read to us, for the television, for the record player, for flowers, for moments such as these in meditation, when in a special way we remember all that God has done for us.

It does us good to come to ourselves, to thank God, and to thank each other, because we are so fortunate. And when we take time to do this we know there will be food and shelter and the care of friends and loved ones when we awake tomorrow. There will be ways, too, that we can reach out through our love for each other and make some other life brighter and more worth living. When that boy came to himself, life took on new meaning. It can happen to us, too.

LIGHT IN DARKNESS
Isaiah 9:2; Matthew 5:14-16; John 1:5

T he author of the Gospel of John was talking about Jesus when he said, "The light shines in darkness, and the darkness cannot put it out." He was boldly proclaiming that our world will never know darkness again, for as Isaiah had prophesied, "the people who walked in darkness had seen a great light." Jesus broke into the dark night of the world and even though the powers of evil and all the forces of darkness attempt to stamp out that light, the light will continue to shine, for the darkness can never overcome it. This is the hope of the world.

You have noticed how penetrating a spark of light is on a dark night. Blackouts during the war were rigidly enforced. It was said that even a burning cigarette might give away the location of a position. How important a spark of light is! One night when my father was driving his team across the Dakota prairie, he lost his way. Suddenly he descended into what he realized was a dry lake bed. He was a preacher with a powerful voice. He called for help and at last he saw a speck of light on the far horizon. That little light showed him the way to safety.

We are familiar with the words of Shakespeare. "How far the little candle throws its beam. So shines a good deed in a naughty world." It was said of Phillips Brooks, that great Boston preacher of the last century, "It was a dull morning until Phillips Brooks came by. As he walked down the street he radiated sunshine and joy." So John said of Jesus, "In him was life and the life was the light of men. The light shines in the darkness and the darkness cannot put it out." Jesus is the "light of the world."

We may recognize Jesus as the light that shines in darkness, but sometimes it is difficult to fit us into the picture, for Jesus added, "You are the light of the world." How do we radiate that light? Just prior to this declaration, Jesus had described what makes us full of light. In the beatitudes (Matthew 5:3-12) he tells what the marks of the blessed people are and what makes them the light of the world. These are among the most inspired sayings in the Scriptures.

Ralph L. Woods tells of an experience that came to John Ruskin.

One evening during the latter part of his life, John Ruskin sat at a window in his home watching a lamplighter, with torch in hand, ignite the street lamps on a distant hill. Since it was dark the lamplighter himself could not be seen, but his progress up the hill could be observed as successive lamps were lighted.

After a few minutes Ruskin turned to a friend and said, "That illustrates what I mean by a genuine Christian. You may not know him or even see him, but his way has been marked by the lights he leaves burning."

Wouldn't it be wonderful if people were to say of us, "His way has been marked by the lights he has left burning."

Soon after I arrived in Bradenton, I heard of a man who was trying to find work. The week before, his wife had left him with three children, the oldest only four. Because he had to take care of the children, he lost the temporary job he had held. Food stamps had been a help; but they were all gone and there would be no more until the next month. He was offered a temporary job at a home near where I was staying. He was most grateful, especially because a neighbor lady offered to care for the children during his hours of work. As I talked with him I could see he had faced darkness, but some who were the light of the world did not let his light go out. We become streetlighters when we have a glow of love in our hearts.

Sometimes it is difficult for us to brighten the day for others because we feel so miserable ourselves. When clouds close in, when our arthritis flares up, when something else throws a shadow over our lives—how hard then to be the light of the world. We may have to settle by being more like the moon, a reflected light, rather than a source of light ourselves. My father used to tell about a man who thought reflected light was indeed important. My father asked him, "Which is the most important, the sun or the moon?" His answer was, "The moon," and he explained it this way. "The moon gives light at night when it is dark. The sun shines in the daytime and there is plenty of light then."

When we are too tired or too sick or too distressed to be lights ourselves, we can still be reflected lights. By reflecting our faith in God, our hopes, our love, darkness cannot put out such light.

Think of all those who have been lights shining for you. There have been many who have helped light my way. There was the little old lady who lived across the street then I was a senior in high school. I had never had a grandmother but she became one for me. In another town there was a Mrs. Craig. I carried out her ashes during the winter, and she would have me sit by the fire where she told me many beautiful and wonderful things. I can't remember what she told me, but I remember the affection she showed me. Then there was Charley Crandle. He was retired and was custodian at the church. He was the gentlest and kindest man I ever knew. These older people, who may have been unaware of their shining lights, were bringing light to a growing boy. They sparked a light in me that I hope will never burn out.

During these moments of quiet meditation we can trim our lamps. God is ready to add his spiritual fuel to our lives. The radiance of faith, the flame of hope, the warmth of love illuminate our lives. "In him was life, and his life was the light of men. His light shines in darkness, and the darkness cannot put it out." We are to let that light shine through our lives until we truly become the light of the world, and Jesus said it would be so.

BE STILL AND KNOW

Psalm 84:1-4, 10-12

The spiritual helps that come to us in meditation and prayer are also found in public worship. The invitation printed below was used, for a time, on the Sunday bulletins for the churches I served in Virginia.

In this period of meditation our minds and hearts pass through a series of responses that prepare us to communicate with God more helpfully. We quiet our minds so we can listen to him. We open our lives to receive his blessing, his comfort, and his power. We rededicate ourselves and seek to know and do his will. And finally we enlarge the compass of our devotion to show compassion to his children everywhere. Now let us share these experiences through meditation and prayer.

> Come, let us worship.
> "Be still and know that I am God."
> Feed your mind on the Truth of God.
> Open your heart to the Love of God.
> Dedicate your will to the Purposes of God.
> Reach out in fellowship and compassion
> to the children of God.

Come Let Us Worship

In worship we take on the nature of the object of our worship. To worship God is to become Godlike or Christlike. In Bulgaria, there is what is called the Valley of the Roses. Field after field are cultivated by the people of the valley. At exactly the right time, they pick the roses so they can extract the oil and make it into perfume that carries the fragrance of the valley around the world. The clothing of the workers is so permeated with this perfume that wherever they go, the air is sweetened and their friends day, "Oh, you have come from the valley of the roses."

Worship is to come into God's presence in such a way that when our period of worship is over, we emerge carrying with us the fragrance, the very evidence, that we have been with God. When we worship we are released from the fetters of self. We are no longer held by a sense of failure. Worship lifts us above our tensions and worries. It does not erase life's trials and errors, but it ties us to God so that together we can face our problems. So it was said of the disciples, "They knew that they had been with Jesus." (Acts 4:13)

"Be Still and Know That I am God"

In the Old Testament we have the story ot Elijah, the prophet of God, who fled from his problems to a cave in the mountains to wait for his death. God passed by, not in the wind or the earthquake or the fire, but in the still small voice—the voice of great stillness. (I Kings 19:9-18) We need to calm our spirits, cool our tempers, alert our faith and trust so God can speak to us in worship.

There was a woman from Ohio who met and married an Englishman. He took her back to England. They could not have children of their own; but they found many waifs who had no homes, so they gathered them into their loving care until there were more than 20 of them. On the first night one of the children was with them, a child they had found on the streets of London, he was heard crying softly; and his new mother took him up in her arms and asked what bothered him. "I'm afraid," he said. All his life he had slept on the streets, under the feet of the traffic of the city, surrounded by constant noise. Here in the quiet of his new home he was away from the familiar sounds of the city and he was afraid. The good mother pulled a mouth organ from her pocket and began to play the quiet music of her childhood. Soon he was quieted. He was in her presence, and he went to sleep. How desperately we need to feel our lives quieted and at peace with God.

Feed Your Minds on the Truth of God

John Greenleaf Whittier's words stir us to a purer worship.

> Dear Lord and Father of mankind,
> Forgive our foolish ways;
> Reclothe us in our rightful mind,
> In purer lives Thy service find,
> In deeper reverence, praise.

"Reclothe us in our rightful mind." In God's presence we get rid of pretenses, half truths, covering up. Our souls stand naked before God, and we can be purified by his forgiving love. We shed false values, false ideas, and feed on his truth that purifies. In God's presence we are humbled. The vast truths of God, his mysterious power, exceed our greatest outreach. The more worthy the saint, the more certain he is that important as is the truth he has found, he has literally only touched the hem of the garment. Here in worship is one place we do reach out for the truth of God. Because we seek it, we will find it.

Open Your Heart to the Love of God

On the Statue of Liberty are words inviting the crushed, the poor, the victims of exploitation, those seeking a new start in life, to come to America. This is a land of hope. I think of worship as being that.

We bring our heartaches, our jealousies, our tempers, our depressions with us. We let the love of Christ wash us clean. We come feeling sorry for ourselves and are given a vision of the world's need so we forget ourselves in service. We come angry with our neighbor and as we wait before God asking him to forgive us—for we are often disobedient children—God's love overflows to include the neighbor who has wronged us.

A description of the Children's Aid Society includes a story of a hardened little girl who lived on the streets of New York. She had been half starved, beaten, sexually molested and terrified. Then came the young woman who was to take the waifs west where they would find new homes on friendly farms. Weeks passed during the difficult train trip carrying the children west. Very slowly love filtered through to the hardened little girl's heart as she found those she could trust. This tenderness of the older woman brought them together one night as the woman drew the child into her arms that she might sleep. Right then it happened. The little waif broke out in tears of gratitude—tears that were the prelude to peaceful slumber. Love overcame her fear and her heartache. We open our hearts to the love of God and our burdens drop away.

We Dedicate Our Wills to the Purposes of God

Abraham Lincoln said words to this effect: It matters little whether God is on our side; it is all important that we are on God's side. Worship is a time to examine ourselves. We do not try to get God's blessing on what is convenient or profitable for us. Rather, we are made ready to readjust our lives to fulfill God's purposes.

A biographer of George Washington Carver tells how at a time when Carver was trying to find money and means to continue his scientific experiments, Thomas A. Edison offered him a high salary to help him develop synthetic rubber from goldenrod. Carver was tempted. Here would be the money he might use in his experiments and indirectly he would be helping humanity. But he decided against it. He had pledged to help the people of the South and particularly his own people, the Blacks. Had God not given him his special gifts and scientific secrets for a greater purpose? He came to a clear decision as he waited before God.

Because we have dedicated our wills to the purposes of God, our decisions are not moments of frustration or crushing disappointment, for God clears the way for what is our ultimate good.

Reach Out in Compassion and Fellowship
To the Children of God

Our communities would be healthier and happier if in some way everyone could be involved in some form of voluntary service. In order to include those who are less able to help others, such a program would have to be carefully planned, but it would generate compassion and provide fellowship, both of which are essential to everyone's well being.

Some years ago an old woman who lived alone in her house admitted she had largely withdrawn from community affairs. She said she was too old, and she had grown too feeble so she was afraid to venture out. In fact, her health was not at all good. Then it was reported that someone must be found to head up a hot-lunch program for the elderly of the community. She thought of all those older people sitting in their living rooms alone and tired. She was about the oldest of the lot, but here was something that challenged her. She was moved with compassion. She decided to volunteer saying that she was tired of being a spectator in a needy world.

That turned her life around. She visited us when she was on a trip from Iowa to Washington and the last I heard she was still the active leader of the group. Compassion and fellowship proved to be her second wind in life.

Worship should alert us to the possibilities of compassion and fellowship. The moment we breathe the words, "Our Father," when we pray the Lord's prayer, we relate to all his children throughout the world. Worship sets our heart-strings vibrating and through the giving of ourselves and what we have, we find a new interest and delight in helping abused children, refugee families, youth programs, and numerous other needy individuals and groups.

Come, then, let us worship. "We kneel so weak, we rise so full of power." Let it be said of us that as we take our places in this busy world, the fragrance and the beauty of the Lord will be evident, for we have been with the Lord our God in meditation and prayer.

HELP ALONG THE WAY

Luke 24:13-26, 45-48

In the scripture reading we find two men hurrying along the road to Emmaeus. They had just passed through a series of traumatic experiences. They were not in that way different than many of us, for such experiences come—the loss of a husband or wife, or a problem that simply crushes us. It may be no more than an irritation, as I discovered when I met a lady the other day and she said, "I'm mad," and she was. Something had gone wrong that upset her. She went about her work until she found a way to iron out her problem; later when I saw her she said her frustration was gone, but it had been a testing time. Whether what bothers us is nearly life-changing or one of those little irritations we have to cope with them.

We would do well to listen to those two men as they walked toward Emmaeus and discover what had happened. They were running away from something. One was saying something like this, "Jesus promised us so much! The day when he said, 'Follow me,' I was ready to leave everything—everything—though my family thought I shouldn't. There was something about him that made me do it."

His companion had been drawn to Jesus in much the same way. "I was won over when he announced, 'The Kingdom of God is at hand.' and he seemed to fulfill all the Law and the Prophets. I felt sure he was the Messiah."

They were silent for a time then one of them asked, "What went wrong? Only a few days ago the crowds shouted Hosannah! Hosannah! when he came to Jerusalem. But many of that same crowd were the ones who called out for Pilate to release Barabbas and crucify Jesus. What had happened? Was it because Jesus went into the Temple and drove out the money changers and cleansed the Temple?"

They walked on; then they began pointing their fingers at those they thought were to blame. "What made Judas decide to sell Jesus for thirty pieces of silver?" But they didn't find much comfort in accusing others; for they remembered that when Jesus had gone to the Garden to pray he had asked someone to watch and pray with him, but they had all gone to sleep. And when the soldiers had come to take him away they had not rushed forward as a group to stand in his defense but had followed afar off. Nor had they done anything when the enemy took Jesus out to be crucified on a hill outside the city, between two thieves.

So now they were running back to Galilee—not on the main road out of Jerusalem, lest they be spotted, but by a round-about way that was relatively safe. They were running to try to escape their problems.

I'm glad there were two of them so that they could talk with each other. It is never wise for us to try to handle our problems without the help others can give. At such times the high privileges of Christian fellowship come into play. It is vital that we seek out those who will understand: a minister, a friend, someone who can offer spiritual strength in our need.

As they went along they overtook a stranger, who, unknown to them, was Jesus. He walked with them and listened, even as he offers to listen when we pour out our needs any time, any place. Jesus then opened up the scriptures and related their problems and perplexities to the whole range of spiritual revelation out of their past. They began to realize there was much that would have helped them if only they had given it thought.

When they reached Emmaeus, they almost lost him, for he said he was going further on; but they urged him to stop with them and, as he broke bread, their eyes were opened. Only then did they know they were with Jesus. Their hearts glowed within them. They recalled how he had opened up the scriptures, and helped them begin to see things differently.

The record says, Jesus vanished out of their sight; but he did not vanish out of their minds and hearts. This encounter turned them around. Only moments before they were running away; now it tells us they ran back to Jerusalem—into the thick of their troubles. There they would renew their fellowship with the others, so they could regroup under the impulse of a tremendous new surge of faith.

The group to which these men returned was no different than other frustrated mortals—weak, unable to understand, wondering what would happen next. Peter was there, who only two nights before had sworn he didn't even know Jesus and then had gone out and wept bitterly. Thomas was there too, who even now doubted that Jesus was alive and was sputtering, "Unless I put my hand into his side. . . ." The others were frightened and were hiding; among them was the mother of Jesus and the other Mary who had gone early to the tomb.

We don't know exactly what happened then, but suddenly Jesus was in their midst and now he threw out a challenge to them. They were to remain right there until they pulled themselves together and until God filled them with his Spirit. Then they were to scatter to the ends of the earth—not to run away; but they were to be so full of power that they would become witnesses of what God does to ordinary mortals who open their lives to him.

Like those early disciples, when we are confronted by perplexities, discouragements, heartaches, and other anxieties, our real hope is that we seek the presence of God or Jesus. It may be through prayer or meditation or fellowship or when reading the scriptures. It will come as we wait before God and our spirits will begin to glow within. Then we, too, will be witnesses, witnesses not to defeat or frustration, but to what can happen when we feed our minds and hearts with his spiritual presence. We will be strong, because we have walked and talked with him along the way and he has turned our lives around.

SYMPATHY

John 13:34, Luke 10:25-37

Today I want you to think about one of the most lovely traits or qualities of an individual—sympathy. Where there is sympathy, life gives off an aroma of tenderness and kindness, of loving thoughtfulness and compassion. Sympathy takes its rise from our highest and best affections and is undergirded by spiritual affirmations that come right out of the very nature of God. The Old Testament writers knew it well. Time after time the psalmists speak of the "lovingkindness" and mercy of God. This comes full orbed in the word "compassion," as when Jesus looked out on the multitude with compassion. This heightened expression of sympathy has its strong spiritual grounding in the words of Jesus. "A new commandment I give unto you, that you love one another." We want to be persons of sympathy. We want that lovely and commanding quality to shine through our lives.

You have noticed, I am sure, that a person who is sympathetic has a certain warmth and charm that naturally draws others to him.

Sympathy is a higher development among human responses. It is a quality that can be cultivated until it gives shape to all of life. Fingers that have never learned the movement and skill of a master violinist are in sharp contrast to those of the artist. After training, the musician's fingers race up and down the strings of a violin, almost faster than the eye can follow. When the master touches the strings and places his fingers with exact skill, he achieves a perfect tone, an exact pitch, a sound of exceptional beauty. A life of sympathy is a trained and skilled life—a life able to let loose the harmonies and sweet music of the soul; best of all it produces this response in both the one who shows sympathy as well as in the one to whom it is shown. In showing sympathy our inmost beings come alive.

In all the teachings of Jesus, probably the best loved parable is of the Good Samaritan. What was it that made the Samaritan the hero of the story? There was much Jesus wanted us to understand when he told that story.

We know that the Samaritans of Jesus' day were somewhat like those of a minority community of our day. In one way or another we allow our prejudices to show through in our treatment of other races or classes. That was the way the Jews regarded the Samaritans. They were never the heroes of Jewish stories. But when Jesus wanted to show an act of sympathy, he chose a Samaritan. Undoubtedly he did this intentionally to bring out the sharp contrast between people who are only superficially good and those who have real worth, and this hinges around this wonderful outpouring sympathy.

There are many characters in the story. The men who beat up the poor traveler obviously were not men of sympathy. But the men who passed him by were not much better, though they should have been. One was a priest. You would expect a priest who is supposed to know much about God to show mercy; but his religion must have been largely professional, or at least he had not cultivated a sympathetic attitude. He passed him by. He was followed by a Levite. Levites were people of a favored class. He may have regarded himself too important to be delayed by an act of kindness. He also passed him by.

Fortunately the Samaritan came along; and though he was on a journey, he stopped to show mercy. He picked him up and took him to an inn where he paid for his care and was willing to do even more.

What made him do it? What are the ingredients of sympathy? There were at least three responses at work in the Samaritan. First, when the Good Samaritan saw the man lying on the road, he must have said, "If I were lying there, what would I want someone to do for me?" When we begin to think that way—to show empathy—we more or less crawl into the other person's problems; and his cry, his hurt, his call for help rises on our lips and touches our hearts. We feel as he feels. That arouses our sympathy.

Edna St. Vincent Millay put this into her poem "Renascence." We can almost feel her agony as she enters into the experience of others.

> All sin was of my sinning, all
> Atoning mine, and mine the gall
> Of all regret. Mine was the weight
> Of every brooded wrong, the hate
> That stood being each envious thrust;
> Mine every greed, mine every lust.
> And all the while for every grief,
> Each suffering, I craved relief
> With individual desire—
> Craved all in vain! And felt fierce fire
> About a thousand people crawl;
> Perished with each—then mourned for all!
> A man was starving in Capri;
> I felt his gaze, I heard his moan,
> And knew his hunger as my own.
> I saw at sea a great fog bank
> Between two ships that struck and sank;
> A thousand screams tore through my throat.
> No hurt I did not feel, no death
> That was not mine; mine each last breath
> That, crying, met an answering cry
> From the compassion that was I.
> All suffering mine, and mine its rod:
> Mine pity like the pity of God.

Then, also, the Samaritan was willing to get involved. In our self-centered ways we tend to say, "It is not our affair." We may even excuse ourselves by saying, "If I were to help, I might get into all kinds of legal trouble." It is true, expressions of sympathy today demand the exercise of caution. We are flooded with appeals on television and through the mail playing on our sympathy. In today's world, sympathy calls for wisdom as well as courage and care, if we are to be involved in the welfare of others. When Jesus taught us to love our neighbor as ourselves, he implied that we should not only attend to the care, protection and welfare of others, but also our own

69

welfare. But this very willingness to be involved gives a person a special quality of outgoing goodness found only among those who are vitally committed to love others as Jesus commanded.

Then also, the Samaritan must have been a person who showed sympathy because he had cultivated that trait throughout his life. He had learned to show sympathy in his home, among his friends, and in his community until that made him a sympathetic man. Practice had perfected this skilled response to the needs of his fellow man.

During my student days, the person often mentioned, who lived out compassion like that of Jesus, was Tohohiko Kagawa of Japan. He was the son of a well-to-do political leader in a rural area. His mother was his father's geisha. Both his father and his natural mother died when he was four and he was raised in a loveless home by his father's real wife. During his youth, he was introduced to Christianity; and at 17 he became a Christian. When he was 21, he came to believe that to be a true Christian he must identify himself completely with those most in need; so he surprised his family and friends by entering the slums of Shinkawa. For the next 20 years he lived most of the time in a six foot square room, often sharing it with beggars, criminals, drifters, and others. His limited income as a chimney sweep went for food and clothing not only for himself, but also for the destitute.

Here was one who did the things he did, because he was the kind of man he was. There was a very practical side to his sympathy. He became the recognized spokesman for the laborers and helped institute labor reforms. He brought about slum clearances and improved housing. He planned and gave shape to the cooperative moment that made food available to multitudes at prices they could pay. His sympathy made him one of the great figures in the uplift of the downtrodden. In time he became a recognized leader in the world Christian community, and when he came to India, he spoke at a great conference that was held in the church of which I was pastor. It was a hallowed experience for me. Just to meet and hear about his sympathic outreach made a profound impression on me and has added to my dedication.

The vital note of sympathy is that we love one another. We have to feel as the Good Samaritan did. We feel the agony, the heartbreak, the pain of another; and it gives a tone and a quality to our lives such as nothing else can.

JONAH

The Book of Jonah

When the thirteenth of the month falls on Friday, there are many who think that before the day is over surely something will go wrong. We associate a character in the Bible, Jonah, with such unexplained mishaps. At such times we say, there must be a Jonah somewhere, and we try to ferret out who or what is causing bad things to happen. Interestingly enough, there is a real story behind all this. It would be well to look at it because we have our modern-day Jonahs; and we call them that because Jonah, in the Bible, was the kind of man he was.

Jonah mirrors many of our feelings and our responses to difficult and demanding situations. We are told that God called him to go to Ninevah where he was to warn the people to repent and straighten up or they would be completely destroyed.

Now Jonah hated the people of Ninevah. He had some justification for his feelings. They had invaded his country, had broken down the walls of his capitol, Samaria, and had taken the great of the city off into captivity in chains. Out of the bitterness of his heart, he didn't want the people of Ninevah to be saved. He wanted them to suffer the wrath of God because they had made his people suffer. So why should he preach to them?

Now Jonah considered himself a very religious man. He prayed regularly to God and down in his heart he probably knew that he should accept God's call and go. There may have been in him something similar to what happens when we repeat the words of the Lord's prayer and say, "Thy Kingdom come, thy will be done, on earth as it is in heaven." We say the words, but we don't stop to think what God's will involves. At most, we have a general feeling that, if we do God's will, we will experience the joy and happiness we associate with the abundant life. We make the same mistake Jonah made. He didn't work out the connection between his prayer life and his obedience to God. His bitter feelings took over and instead of going to Ninevah, he took a boat and went as fast as he could in the opposite direction. He headed for Tarshish.

Jonah didn't find much peace on the boat. It was loaded with all sorts of things, and he didn't have a reserved stateroom. Then the boat ran into a storm and was about to sink. To save the boat, the sailors threw the cargo overboard and still they were about to go down. In their desperation, they began accusing each other, saying, someone has surely displeased his god. Their only hope was to find out who the guilty person was and throw him overboard. That sent Jonah into hiding all the more, but finally they found him and said, "You must be our troublemaker. You must be our Jonah." Poor fellow, he had to admit that he was in the very act of escaping from his God—that he simply would not go and preach repentance to the people of Ninevah.

That was all the sailors needed to know. Overboard went Jonah. We hear no more about the boat and its crew; apparently they arrived safely. But we take up the story of Jonah. Evidently he was almost glad to be tossed overboard. He accepted his fate. He would rather be dead than see his enemy repent and be saved. His hard-heartedness has a familiar ring.

When Jonah hit the water, he probably thought, "Now, I won't have to go to Ninevah." But the writer makes clear that God wasn't done with him yet. He explained that God caused a big fish to swallow Jonah, and after three days the fish deposited Jonah back on dry land, not far from where he had started. Again the call came, "Now go, tell those evil people in Ninevah to repent. I want to save them."

All that sounds familiar, too. We try desperately to get out of doing God's will, when it cuts across our pet prejudices and dispositions. We may succeed to escape for a time, but eventually God catches up with us. We don't shed many tears over people we strongly dislike, just as we note was true of Jonah, and we not all too secretly wish they would feel the fury of God and things would go wrong for them. How determined we seem to be to pass over the import of the words we use when saying the Lord's prayer, "Forgive us our trespasses as we forgive those who have trespassed against us." I wonder if it ever occurred to Jonah that God was offering him salvation, too, and that his soul was in the balance, until he got over his hatred for the people of Ninevah.

There is more to the story. Now that Jonah was on dry land, he had to so something about God's call. This time he went to Ninevah and preached as he had been commanded. What a preacher he must have been, for the people of Ninevah repented—thousands and thousands of them.

That should have made Jonah happy. He might even have boasted a bit and said, "Praise God. Now I have accomplished your will. The people have repented." But that didn't happen. Jonah, we discover, was a small person. He was selfish and stubborn. He had made up his mind that the people of Ninevah should be destroyed and not even God himself could change his mind. He hadn't wanted to preach to them, and now since they had repented, he was angry; and he prayed, reminding God, how such compassion went against everything he stood for. "I knew that thou art a gracious God and merciful, slow to anger, and abounding in steadfast love, and repentest of evil." That, he said, was the reason he had run away in the first place and tried to go to Tarshish. But here he was. Ninevah had repented and the people were saved. That was more than Jonah could bear, so in despair and anger, he said, "Therefore now, O Lord, take my life from me, I beseech thee, for it is better for me to die than to live."

He didn't get his way in that, either. Instead, God tried to soften him and show mercy on him. God made a further effort to arouse Jonah's better nature. His last word for Jonah was, "Should I not pity Ninevah, that great city in which there are more than a hundred and twenty thousand persons. . . . ?" Not even God could appeal to Jonah's pity or cause him to show mercy. That is enough to make him a Jonah—one who brings misfortunes in any situation. He is one character in the Bible with whom no one wants to be identified.

We can learn our lessons from Jonah. We learn that when one goes against the will of God, he becomes a Jonah, adding to the problems and anxieties of the world. We learn, too, that the mercy and goodness of God overrides the most stubborn and hard-hearted among us. In spite of man's rebellion, in spite of the Jonah in each of us, God continues to strive for man's redemption and salvation, even a poor sinner and disobedient person such as Jonah.

OUT OF THE VALLEY

Psalm 23

These moments of meditation help us feel God's presence in a special way. In our solitary moments questions come to us that we hesitate to voice even among a circle of close and understanding friends. One question that puzzles many and has been asked as long as we have records of the way man has thought, is this, "Why did a good and loving God make a world in which there is suffering? Why should we be afflicted with problems and sometimes experience disasters?"

In this brief meditation, you wouldn't expect me to come up with anything like a complete answer, but there are some thoughts that I would like to share with you. Some are drawn from what Dr. Arthur Caliandro wrote when giving his advice on "What to do when life says no."

We begin this answer with a reference to the writings of Stephen Neill. Neill was for a time a missionary in India whom I was privileged to know. Neill points out that problems, anxieties, hardships, and the like come to people everywhere. Evil and suffering will never entirely go away. As long as we live we will have to face such problems and difficulties. But Neill says, we should ask a more helpful question—"Why did God choose to make a dangerous world? God must have had a reason to make a world in which there is tragedy and suffering."

He believes that God has put us in this kind of a world because he wants us to grow. Life is so designed that we will not grow unless we face and overcome problems. God wants us to be strong, and we can only become strong, intelligent, compassionate, and tender when we overcome our problems. By overcoming them we grow into strong personalities.

Think, for instance, how a child learns to walk. I have seen children in India well over two years old who could hardly take a step. During those months of growth, if the child cried, his mother would pick him up, straddle him on her hip, and go about her work. When he is old enough to be running and playing, such a child can hardly stand. His legs are weak and thin. He has been carried all his life. He was not allowed to fall and get up and struggle in a normal way. So he hasn't become strong; he hasn't matured; he is still a baby. Hard knocks, spills, trying time after time helps him to become a real person. In

74

order for him to learn to walk he has to face the problems involved in walking.

A flute player who rides with me on the way to a band in which I play in Sarasota, is all excited about new techniques he is learning from his teacher. This former Superintendent of Schools, at 68, tells that the sweet music of the flute has been his problem. Now, he says, it is beginning to come at last. Any musician, dancer, actor, technician, inventor, teacher, or ordinary man or woman grows strong, and his character takes shape, as he overcomes his problems. That is the only way we can ever grow, to say nothing of becoming sweet and loving.

In the 23rd Psalm, the psalmist begins with the wonderful affirmation, "The Lord is my Shepherd, I shall not want." That may be all we need for faith. But in the fourth verse he goes on, "Yea, though I walk through the valley of the shadow of death, I will fear no evil, for thou art with me." This is often thought of as a verse of comfort at the time of death, but there is more. As the psalmist says, "Though I walk though the valley. ..." Here are our problems, our valleys, our depressions, our difficult relationships. We have to walk through them. They help built us up, because, as the psalmist says, we should fear no evil for God is with us. Each situation is such that it can add new dimensions to our characters. With God's help, nothing can happen to us that cannot become a means of growth to make our lives beautiful.

One of the secrets of growth, when we face a problem, is to view it not as a blank wall, the end, the final and unsurmountable roadblock, but look at it as the end of one phase of our lives and an open door to something new. It was Phillips Brooks, one of the great preachers of the last century, who said, "Life is full of ends, but every end is a new beginning." This is especially important for us as we grow older.

How do we handle our new beginnings? There will likely come a time when many of my readers will have to move from their private homes into what at first seems to be very cramped quarters. The adjustments seem almost over-powering. But before long, if there is a willingness to adjust, the new life is found to have its rewards. We might prefer it if there would come a time when we are not called on to make adjustments, but this is not a real possibility. The secret is to learn how to turn an end, a blank wall, into a new beginning. Changes involve forming new friendships, new ways to reach out a helping hand, but as this happens, the discovery comes, that our environment isn't so important but it is increasingly important to turn our problems into stepping stones for something better. It is dangerous to accept a change as a dead end, rather the end of one lifestyle must prove to be the beginning of a new.

Our faith tells us that even death itself is not an end but a new beginning. When our life on earth ceases, then we are free of our frail bodies. Our spirits are eternal, and we are ushered into a whole new realm of experiences. One of my friends has often remarked, "I just wish there had been a television crew present when Jesus brought Lazarus from the grave and recorded his first-hand report of what life beyond death had been like." Yes, even the end of life is no blank wall but a new beginning.

So we live in a world that has its problems, its trials. These give shape and add dignity and poise and a glow to our lives as we learn how to handle them with God's help. We are precious in his sight. We become precious to each other as we give evidence that the hardships of life have matured and blessed us and helped us become the really loving person God wants us to be.

WHAT IS IN YOUR HAND?

John 6:1-14, Matthew 25:34ff.

Most everyone today knows of the beautiful painting of the praying hands of Albrecht (Albert) Dürer. It was almost five centuries ago he painted them. The hands have been reproduced in many art forms: as models, in sculpture, and in other forms of art. Seeing them reminds us of God's nearness and also stirs in us other emotions. Hands have reached out to touch our lives—the hands of parents, of friends, of companions, of teachers, of ministers, and many others.

One moment stands out above others as I think of those hands. We were together in a great Christian student gathering in Kandy, Ceylon (Sri Lanka) at Christmas, 1940. Students had come from all over southern Asia. We were standing, as was the custom in the Orthodox Church, during a three hour service. At the moment when our hallelujahs had been sung and our hearts were over-flowing, the minister-in-charge asked us to give "the kiss of peace." We faced those nearest us and with our hands held much as we see them in the painting, we folded our hands over theirs and then they, in turn, covered our hands with theirs. As our hands touched in that way, students from different countries, speaking different languages, following different forms of worship, suddenly felt united together in the very presence of God. God seemed to reach out and touch us as we touched each other.

You probably have seen Dürer's picture of the praying hands, but have you heard the story behind that painting? Albert Dürer was the son of a goldsmith living in Nuremburg, Germany. As a boy, he always wanted to draw and paint, but he had to work long hours at his father's trade. It was not until he was grown that his parents permitted him to go away and study with a great artist. But it was not easy. He had to support himself so there was little time for his art. After a time he found a friend, somewhat older, who was also struggling to become an artist. They decided to live together to save money, but they remained so desperately poor that the friend finally suggested that for a time he would give up his studies so he could earn more and in that way, by pooling their income, they could manage. They planned that as soon as Dürer began to earn from his art, his friend would begin his studies again.

They lived in this way for some years, Dürer studying and his friend working. At last Dürer created a carving that earned him enough so they were both able to study again. But when his friend took up his brush he soon saw that his hands had become stiff. The joints were enlarged; he could not hold his brush as he should, and there was no help for him. He had to give up his hopes of ever becoming an artist.

Dürer was broken-hearted and resolved to care for his friend the rest of his life. One day when he returned to his room, he heard his friend at prayer. He looked over and saw those hands reverently folded. "I can never give him back his skill," Dürer said, "but I can show the world the depth of his love for me and my love for him. I will paint his hands as they are folded in prayer. When people see his worn hands, they will remember with what love and devotion others have toiled for them, and like me, express in some beautiful way their gratitude for such loving service."

As you look at your hands, you could well ask, "What kind of a story do they tell? Are they hands of service? Have they toiled to bring hope and joy to others?"

One of the remarkable lessons of our Christian faith is that God can take our hands, or what is in our hands, and miracles begin to happen. An incident recorded in the Gospel of John tells of a boy who was seen at the edge of the crowd. Jesus had been teaching the multitude, and it was time for them to eat. The disciples informed Jesus they had nothing to give them, nor did they have money to buy food for such a crowd. Jesus sent word and asked the boy what he had in his hand and the boy offered what he had. With the loaves and fishes, Jesus fed the multitude. He used what was at hand to perform one of his noblest deeds. We do not fully know what happened but it was one of the many examples of how God takes what is in one's hands and almost immediately what seem like miracles begin to happen. That is the way God works.

There was Moses. The Israelites were slaves in the land of Egypt. God asked, "What is in your hand, Moses?" Moses replied, "A rod." God told him to use it, and because God worked through Moses, the sea opened to let the Israelites go over. Moses struck the rock at the mountain, and it gave forth a spring of water. The people had been slaves in Egypt and were ill-prepared to conquer their former homeland. Moses turned them into conquerors so that they could go in and possess the land. God used what was in Moses' hand.

What is in your hand, David? Only a slingshot? Not for a moment did David think he was acting in his own might, but what the armies of Israel had failed to do, a boy with a slingshot in his hand did with God's help. He delivered his nation from the hands of the Philistines.

What is in your hand? Do you reach out and touch others in compassion? Is there kindness, helpfulness, mercy in your hand? When you touch others do you bring them joy?

Jesus was much interested in what we do with what is in our hands. In Matthew 25 we read the description of the day of judgement.

> The King will say to those on the right hand, "Come, O blessed of my Father, inherit the kingdom prepared for you from the foundation of the world; for I was hungry and you gave me food, I was thirsty and you gave me drink, I was a stranger and you welcomed me, I was naked and you clothed me. I was sick and you visited me, I was in prison and you came to me." Then the righteous will answer him, "Lord, when did we see thee hungry

and feed thee, or thirsty and gave thee drink? And when did we see thee sick or in prison and visit thee?" And the king will answer them, "Truly, I say to you, as you did it to one of the least of these my brethren, you did it to me."

"Come, you blessed of the Father," you have used what is in your hand to bless others and this is pleasing in God's sight. When we see Dürer's painting, or when we look at our own hands, we are reminded that God can take whatever is in our hands and right then the miracle of tender love, compassion, kindness, and generosity begins. God uses our hands to let loose powers and responses for good that cannot be measured. And the king will say, "Come, O blessed of my Father, inherit the kingdom prepared for you from the foundation of the world."

ENDURANCE

I Corinthians 9:24-27

When we think of endurance, it is natural to associate it with a person who runs a race. A marathon, where thousands compete, includes some who run the first mile fast; then have to drop out because they are exhausted. There are others who set a steady pace and continue on to the finish. Some even appear to grow fresher and more able to compete as they get into their stride. Endurance is a valuable part of life.

Now I have observed that some of the most courageous examples of endurance are to be found among the elderly. They do not jog. They may not try to outdistance others. In some ways they are held captive to the aging process. Because of age they will never again do many of the lively things they once did, or move as freely in the wide sweep of activities that marked their younger years. But just as each runner in the marathon, so each older person has to decide how he or she will run life's race. Also, like the runner, they learn they can increase their power of endurance as they build up their physical and spiritual powers. All of us are eager to include in our lifestyle the enduring qualities that enable us to run a winning race. Like all others we must learn the secret of enduring, day by day.

One of the first things a person does in preparation for a race is to learn all he can about endurance. Our kind of race calls for certain attitudes and guidelines that are strikingly illustrated in a little book, *The Manhood of the Master*, by Dr. Harry Emerson Fosdick. In it he tells how Jesus and others endured when they were faced with the high demands of courageous living.

The first thing we should realize is that not we alone but everyone has to live under some handicap or other. We weaken ourselves when we fall into the trap of making allowances or excuses for ourselves. It is easy to say that if we did not have our handicap, or if we had money, or if we had better health, or if only we did not have to carry a terrible sorrow, or under different circumstances, or at a different time, or. ... Such matters need not dictate our responses, for we, like others, can bend those circumstances for our welfare when we exhibit "patience, courage, persistant faith, and fortitude."

Look at the gospels. There was no self-pity as Jesus met his unideal situations. He met them so bravely we hardly think of them as being unideal, yet they were. Jesus had reasons to be discouraged. He tried constantly to communicate God's love, but often he was misunderstood. (Mark 13:13-15) He tried to teach his disciples to be humble, but two of them became involved in a squabble about who should have the highest honors in the Kingdom. (Mark 10:35-41) Near the end of his life, the religious leaders and the Roman officials mocked him and gave him over to be crucified. And there were not only these outer struggles, there was the inner one as well. We hear him say, "Now is my soul troubled; and what shall I say? Father, save me from this hour." Surely his agony was great. A moment later he found the strength to say, "But for this cause came I unto this hour. Father, glorify thy name." (John 12:27ff.)

Yes, we would conclude, as Dr. Fosdick did, "His life sounds a courageous call to all of us: Stop whining; stop pitying yourself; see what you can do, by the help of God, with your unideal situation, for God never would have given it to you without some fine possibilities in it."

But there is not particular strength in the discovery that like everyone else we have unideal situations. The next step is to realize that, with the help God is ready to give us, we can take even unideal situations and turn them into triumph. A short poem tells of a fierce battle that is in progress. A prince, who leads a company of soldiers, finds himself completely surrounded by the enemy; and he fights desperately along-side his men. The battle is going badly. At a distance a weak and timid soldier looks on cowardly and says, "If only I had the prince's sword, I would turn the battle to victory," and so saying, he throws down his blunt sword and creeps from the field. Then the center of conflict shifts to where the weak solider once stood. By then the prince, desperately wounded and swordless, sees the broken blade lying in the dust. He snatches it up and "with battle-shout. ... saved a great cause that heroic day." Courageously we can take an unideal situation, comparable to the blunt sword which the timid soldier cast down, and laying hold of the power God gives us, we can turn a most unideal situation into something good for us and for others.

We may have to go a step further. We may not learn to endure until we are prepared to give up something of our comfort to assure the welfare of others. Herein we begin to grow a character. Dr. Fosdick rightly observes, "Nothing is as powerful as love that is willing to suffer." When we look at Jesus' endurance we see this as one of his outstanding qualities. Love motivated his every breath. He did not count the cost. Likewise we will surely find that we will exhibit our greatest strength when we, acting within our limitations, reach out to help others. We should covet this experience, for it adds a remarkable quality to our lives.

Lastly, there is nothing that contributes more to our endurance than a sure confidence that, as Paul said, "All things work together for good." An endurance built on that trustful confidence is not dumb resignation but a deliberate focusing the resources and power God gives us so we not only endure, our endurance takes on a distinctly measurable quality. Jesus exhibited this. He had a powerful presence because of his dependence on God. He was poised and in command at all times. Nothing, even his enemies, daunted him. He was confident in God. Dr. Fosdick is right. It enabled him to "endure courageously, sacrifice freely, labor hopefully," and it will do the same for us.

So how do we handle unideal situations? How able are we to endure? The same heartbreaks and problems that turn some bitter and make them angry and resentful, may mellow others. Such difficulties bring out what is on the inside; and that is the reason we need to rely more on God, to generate spiritual powers that help us endure. It is gratifying to know that we can, with the help of God, handle unideal situations in ways that will make us kinder, more compassionate, and give us the strength and joyful calm that belongs to those who trust God. Look around you and observe for yourself. Some of the most courageous examples of endurance are to be found among those whose only apparent source of endurance is their faith in God.

AWAKENING TO BEAUTY

Philippians 3, 4; Psalm 19

On my first trip to India in 1935, we stopped at the Botanical Gardens in Breitenzorg, Java (Indonesia) where, for the first time I saw giant water lilies. According to my diary, some of the leaves measured several feet across. Rising over them were the beautiful flowers, some pure white, others pink or lavender, mingled with other pastel shades, and in the center of each flower, a bit of yellow to set off all the rest in a vision of beauty.

The lily puts its roots down to the bottom of the pond and draws nourishment from the muck and mud lying there. The oozy, slimy muck, that by itself gives off a terrible odor, provides the food that the plant transforms into great beauty.

A poet has written, "In the mud and scum of things, there's always, always something sings." St. Paul was aware of the muck. In his letter to the Philippians, he writes, "Look out for the dogs, look out for the evil-workers, look out for those who mutulate the flesh." But he saw a Christian community rising in beauty above its evil surroundings and urged them to let that beauty rule their lives. "Finally, brethren," he wrote, "Whatever is true, whatever is pure, whatever is lovely, whatever is gracious, if there is any excellence, if there is anything worthy of praise, think on these things."

We must tune our lives both to see beauty and to let that beauty shine through. On my way to India during the war, I travelled with Dr. Ralph Stewart, a great botanist from the Punjab (then one of the States of India). In Cape Town, South Africa, we went to the Botanical Gardens and Museum where Dr. Stewart was known because he had sent specimens to them from the Punjab. As we went through the Gardens, we saw the beautiful crepe myrtle bushes, loaded with bloom. I decided right then to take some of it with me to

India, so we could have it on our College campus. I really didn't know what I was getting myself in for. I carefully packed some tender plants with Dr. Stewart's advice and kept them watered and protected on that extended trip. First there was the train trip from Cape Town to Durban, followed by a delay there until I could get passage to India. Then, for weeks we were in convoy, moving at four knots an hour, up the east coast of Africa to Mombassa, Kenya. After our delay there we took ship again for India; and once on land again, I took a train to the center of that sub-continent. It was a miracle but I arrived with the crepe myrtle still alive and showing signs that it would survive.

Imagine my surprise, when I arrived on the campus, holding my plants so carefully, to discover that the campus was alive with crepe myrtle. It was everywhere and had been all the years I had lived there, but I had never seen it until my eyes were opened to its beauty in South Africa. "In the mud and scum of things, there's always, always something sings," but we have to open our eyes to see its beauty.

Dr. William Stidger tells of a letter he received in response to a radio broadcast. A mother wrote that she had taken her two children for a walk in the park. As they rested for a moment on a park bench, a crippled old woman came by holding two or three somewhat wilted wildflowers she had picked. She hobbled along but when she saw the children, she stopped and a smile flooded her face. The smile revealed she had only one or two teeth, and the mother looked at the pathetic creature with compassion. Then the old woman handed her flowers, one by one, to the children, and turned and went on her way. This act of kindness moved the youngest to turn to her mother and with a rapture in her voice say, "Mother, wasn't she beautiful!"

How grateful I am that people draw my attention to things of beauty. One day when I stopped at the side of a lady in a wheel chair, she took my hand and, pointing to some large, old trees, said, "Those trees are so beautiful." Another, when I stood near her bed, held a rose in her hand and told me how those roses continue to open, bit by bit, and continue giving off their perfume. How grateful she was for that beautiful rose. There are other things of beauty; a loving touch, a smile, a kind word, a helpful deed. These special graces are ways to help others discover God's beauty. They become the joy and delight, both to the one who is beautiful, and to the one who sees. And when day is done and the lights are low, so you cannot see with your physical eyes, remember the words of St. Paul, "Whatever is true, whatever is pure, whatever is lovely, whatever is gracious, if there is any excellence, if there is anything worthy of praise, think on these things."

Prayer. O God, you touch the rose with color, perfume, and beauty of form. It opens to your sunshine and rain. It keeps on changing day by day as it matures, giving out its fragrance and beauty. Visit us during this time of meditation and prayer, to give color and shape, freshness and loveliness to our minds, hearts, and souls. You touch us in our need, and these moments of communion with you make our faith strong as we are uplifted by your love. Now we place ourselves in your care so we may receive a spiritual miracle that adds beauty and loveliness to our lives. Amen.

THE SIMPLE SOLUTION

II Kings 5:1-14

Everyone likes a good drama. Drama involves heroes and heroines mixed in suspense and conflict. There are always the good guys and the bad guys, and all the time we are waiting to find out who is going to win out in the end. Drama holds our interest because we get involved, hoping and trusting that everything will come out all right when it is all over.

The drama we will think of today was not written by a Shakespeare or a great writer, but is simply told. It is about Naaman, the commander of the armies of the king of Syria, and how he was cured of his leprosy. The whole drama is beautifully told in a few verses in the book of II Kings. We need to read it for ourselves.

The characters attract our attention. There was Naaman, himself. He was not only a captain of the king of Syria, but he acted like a captain. When he gave an order, he expected his men to jump and obey. Also, he enjoyed the special favor of his king, and the writer tells us that God had especially favored him with victory over his enemies. On one of his raids against the Israelites, he had taken many captives, and among them was another of the important characters, a little girl, who became a handmaiden to the captain's wife. We are never told her name.

There was something remarkable about this little girl. She had been raised in the Hebrew faith; her family had apparently surrounded her with such love that, when she discovered that Naaman had leprosy, she forgot her anger and resentment because of what had happened to her, and her heart went out to help her master. She was especially brave, because Naaman and his household worshipped other gods, but she had the courage to tell about her God who was a God of compassion. She even told what Naaman would have to do if he were to get the help he needed from her God. He would have to go see the prophet, Elisha, and then he would be cured.

Elisha, another of our characters, was a man of God and was known as a fearless prophet. But before we say anything about him, we should take a look at the two kings. In this drama, the king of Syria is shown to be the more pleasant of the two. When Naaman went to him, he offered to write to the king of Israel to arrange for Naaman to visit the prophet and be cured. Apparently he cared greatly for his loyal officers.

The king of Israel doesn't show up as well. He is seen as a jealous, suspicious, and unkind fellow who thought the worst of the king of Syria and probably of Naaman, too. When Naaman came with the letter from his king, the king of Israel threw a fit, tore off his clothes, and pouted as only a king can.

Elisha got wind of what was happening. He reminded his king that it would be a feather in their caps if together they could show the king of Syria that their God could effect a cure for leprosy. To simplify matters, he said, "Just send him to me, let him know that there is a prophet in Israel."

There is still one more character we must mention, but first, let us follow the drama. We see Naaman arriving at the palace loaded with gifts and the letter from his king. That was when the king of Israel threw a fit. We aren't told, but I presume the king kept all the gifts and after he had pouted a while, he sent Naaman on to Elisha.

Elisha probably lived in a very simple place. It must have been quite a sight to see Naaman with his horses and chariots draw up in front of Elisha's door. Elisha wasn't that much impressed. He didn't rush out and throw himself on the ground, as an inferior often did with such a great captain. Rather, Elisha sent a servant out to deliver his message. "Go and wash in the Jordan seven times, and your flesh will be restored, and you shall be clean."

Then the drama comes alive. Naaman fumed. He was insulted, first, because the prophet had not shown him proper respect. Second, Naaman took Elisha's instructions to wash in the Jordan as a national insult. He declared that the rivers of Syria were as clear and curative as the Jordan, so why should he not wash in one of them? But the third reason was the most dramatic; and it is in this connection we are introduced briefy to Naaman's servant, the last character of the drama.

Naaman had said that the least Elisha should have done was to come out of his house and wave his hand over the leprosy to heal it in a miraculous way. Such a simple thing as to wash in the river Jordan was a clear insult. Saying this, he was about to return home in a rage when his servant intervened and proved to be wiser than his master. "My father," he said, "if the prophet had commanded you to do some great thing, would you not have done it? How much rather, then, when he says, 'Wash and be clean.'"

The servant was persuasive. Naaman did wash and was cleansed, and the two wisest and most helpful in the whole drama were the little girl and the servant. One had expressed her faith in God, and the other had said in effect, "Don't try to tell God what to do. Sometimes what may appear to be the simplest solution may be the best."

As I have thought of this drama, I can see that it is trying to say something to us today. The drama of our lives shows that sometimes we expect someone to wave a wand over whatever is wrong and "pronto" it disappears. And haven't we all heard people say, "I'd give anything to get rid of this headache," or, "I'd give anything to be able to walk or talk just like I used to." That's what Naaman had said, he'd do anything to get cured, but when he was asked to do a simple thing, he balked.

The simplest solution very often is, "Get involved." You have probably been told to exercise to help tired muscles come alive. You have been invited to share in games and activities that stimulate the mind and rekindle social graces. You have craved friendship as a cure for loneliness, and have been told that the only way to have a friend is to be one. You have said that you would spend more time in meditation and prayer so that you might tune your spirit to God's. All these are so simple, yet the most helpful cures are most often the simple ones.

We need to remember the whole cure began with that little slave girl. There were reasons why she could have been resentful and angry. She might have struck out in hatred to get even with Naaman for what he had done to her. Rather she showed human kindness. God had touched her life so she rose above bitterness to help someone who was suffering. Kindness can become a dramatic quality in every one of us.

All this is drama. That little girl who had the love of God flowing through her life started a chain reaction that not only reshaped the lives of those around her, but reaches down across three thousand years to spark our emotions. It excites us. It tells us that we can apply God's simplest solutions to whatever is the "leprosy" of our lives today.

PEACE OF MIND

Philippians 2:1-6, 4:8f.

Much has been written in recent years about peace of mind, and such peace is said to be present when one's mind is not disturbed, agitated, or frustrated, but is in control—in harmony with the universe. Some think of it as a mind so shut off from the troubles and conflicts of life that it can be compared to a ship at anchor in a quiet harbor. But there is a better description of what I have in mind. The scene is a waterfall with the torrent thundering over the ledge. Below is a tree at the edge of the spray with the thundering water splashing near its branches. In the fork of the tree is a nest where a mother bird has laid her eggs and hatched her young. In what might seem a hostile environment she is peacefully feeding her young, surrounded by the thundering fury of the waterfall.

Such was the peace we see in Jesus the night before he was crucified. After Judas had left the Upper Room and Jesus was fully aware that his enemies were about to strike, he told his disciples, "Peace I leave with you, my peace I give to you. ... Let not your hearts be troubled, neither let them be afraid." How desperately we need such peace of mind. It would be well to look more deeply for the secret that can unlock it for us in our need.

As we follow Jesus through that night of trial, he did not lose his composure. He had peace of mind for he was in tune with the will of God. In the midst of conflict he was not a victim but the master of every situation. He was not a chip floating on a sea of enmity, but while his disciples fled or denied him, and while Pilate and the other authorities were uncertain and washed their hands, Jesus' mind was composed. He drew on spiritual and mental powers that seemed to thwart the brutal will of his enemies, and, because his mind was filled with peace, he endured the agony of body that accompanied their actions when they stripped him of his clothing and beat and mocked him. His mind and his spirit were in control throughout that ordeal. He was sustained by a law of life that is in effect for everyone of us. Our minds and our spirits can take over so that, whatever comes to us, we may be able to meet it because we fix our minds on the resources of strength available for our lives.

Did not the Apostle Paul have this in mind when he said, "Have this mind in you which was in Christ Jesus. ... Set your mind on things above and not on things below. ... For as a man thinketh in his heart, so is he."

We are expected to harness our minds for our health and our happiness. We can have such peace of mind, but it isn't ours by accident any more than was the peace Jesus knew. What was the source of his peace of mind? Can we discover those sources of peace and draw on them for ourselves?

First, Jesus was aware that, as the song writer puts it, "This is my Father's world. ... All nature sings, and round me rings the music of the spheres." He saturated his mind with the presence of God everywhere—the birds of the air, the lilies of the field, the grass which today is and tomorrow is cast into the oven, the grain, the mustard seed, the salt, the light, the leaven in a lump of dough. Fishermen, shepherds, a woman caught in adultery, a multitude without food, the child, the sick with palsy, the widow and her mite, were part of God's world. All these spoke to him of God and he nurtured his mind and spirit on evidences of God all about him. He called those whose minds were closed to such awareness of God, "men of little faith." (Matthew 6:25-33) Like a perfectly tuned instrument giving out its harmonies, so Jesus tuned his mind and soul to evidences of God in the world about him.

88

Second, his mind was open to stirring impressions, and he found a high example of this in children. He took a child and put him in the midst of his followers and said, "Unless you become as little children, you cannot enter the Kingdom of Heaven." He was not upholding childishness or tempermental responses or petty selfishness. Rather he saw in children their ability to grow, to open their lives to great thoughts and new ideas and to respond to endless opportunities. Life, as Jesus understood it, was to be exciting, eager, and trusting.

The mind of Christ stimulates growth. He prompts us to reach out for knowledge, truth, and for sympathetic understanding. We reject all that narrows and limits life. Each of us should expect nothing less than "the abundant life." In this, Jesus offers a positive source of peace of mind.

Third, Jesus knew his traditions. He was not a slave to the past, but he turned his alert and creative mind to grasp moral and spiritual insights of the Prophets and the leaders of his race. So he could take the laws of the past and give them effective meaning for his generation. "You have heard it said of old time, you shall love your neighbor and hate your enemy, but I say unto you, love your enemy and pray for them that persecute you." (Matthew 5:43f.)

Peace is possible only when each generation can use its wisdom to enlarge the borders of human understanding so that the petty conflicts within our minds and hearts as well as the communal strife that has set nation against nation may be overcome in the spirit of the one who came to bring "peace on earth, goodwill among men."

Fourth, Jesus looked for the good in the most unlikely places. Matthew, who later was to write a Gospel, was formerly a tax collector for the hated Romans. Fellow Jews spoke of him as one among the Publicans and sinners and warned Jesus against any contact with him. Jesus looked beyond appearances and saw potential. He had a way of touching life on a low level and lifting it to a high. The Gospels are full of such transformations, "For the Son of Man came not to destroy men's lives but to save them." (Luke 9:56) A strong, positive reliance on the good pervaded all he said and did. This emphasis became a "set" of his mind and spirit. Truly he was the "light of the world," and when he touched lives he released their light so that the darkness could not put it out. (John 1:5)

Fifth, he had a mind that was steadfast and true. Religious leaders of his day misrepresented him and turned people against him. But he acted positively; he did not react negatively or defensively.

Hardly a day passes when we do not react negatively. We make judgments or speak of others in ways that compromise our moral integrity. We have negative feelings and denounce others, because they are black or yellow or brown. We cheat a little. We close our eyes to such things as the constant portrayal of violence, drunkenness, and blatent sexuality on television. We allow our minds to be weak and helpless. Often we react in a festering way while it was Jesus' way to act positively, as Paul later put it, to "overcome evil with good." (Romans 12:21) His mind was steadfast and true and ours can be, too.

Peace of mind, then, is not peace for lack of conflict but a grounding of the mind and spirit that makes us like a house built on a rock. The house built on sand fell when the storm came. The house on the rock did not escape the storm, but it stood because it was built on a rock. (Matthew 7:24-27)

The delightful part of all this is that when Jesus offered this peace of mind it was not just for the young who had a whole life in which they could put all the ingredients of peace together. Many of his followers were advanced in years. When Jesus touches life, of whatever age, peace of mind takes over. We can have peace of mind if we want it. Paul said, "Have this mind in you which was in Christ Jesus. Set your minds on things above and not on things below. . . . For as a man thinketh in his heart, so is he."

LIVE AND HELP LIVE
Mark 8:27-38; Matthew 25:34ff.

What exactly did Jesus mean when he said, "If any man would come after me, let him deny himself, take up his cross and follow me. . . . Whoever would save his life will lose it and whoever loses his life for my sake and the gospel's will save it."

These verses have troubled me. On another occasion Jesus said that he had come to bring life and bring it more abundantly. (John 10:10) Is this charge to deny ourselves, contradictory? What exactly did he mean when he asked us to take up our crosses? How can we save our lives by losing them? How can we be sure that if we lose our lives for

Christ's sake and the gospel's, we will be saving them? Does this add up to the abundant life?

I recently witnessed a scene that suggested at least part of the answer. The parents of a little Mary (not her real name), who live nearby, bought her a badminton set and soon it was set up so they could play. The net, the rackets, the shuttlecocks were all there. About that time three neighbor children rushed onto the court and took up the rackets, positioning themselves to play the game. Right then Mary let out a loud scream and between her tears she commanded them to put down the rackets, saying, "Put them down, put them down. Those rackets are mine." Of course the neighbor children were confused and made their protests, but before long they put the rackets down and slowly returned to their own yard. Then it was that we saw Mary standing at the net, holding her racket to her breast, tears streaming down her face. She had just discovered that her new game could not really be hers unless and until she shared it.

John Wesley said that about religion. "There is no solitary religion." Religion involves others. "He who would save his life must lose it." Mary learned she had to lose sole possession of her rackets in order to play the game. The same is true in the game of life in all our relationships.

Everyone must learn this truth sooner or later. Dr. Albert Schweitzer of Lambarene, Africa, struggled to understand it. On October 13, 1905, when he was pastor of a Lutheran congregation in Alsace, he wrote about that struggle.

> Many times I tried to settle what meaning lay hidden for me in the saying of Jesus, 'Whoever would save his life shall lose it, and whosoever shall lose his life for my sake and the gospel's shall save it.' Now I found the answer and found an inward happiness that surpassed my outward happiness.

What meaning did this saying have for him? Not only was he pastor of a congregation, but he was also head of a seminary where he taught young ministers, as they prepared for Christian service. Furthermore he had already become a major figure in the field of philosophy and had earned doctoral degrees in both philosophy and theology. Added to this was his outstanding achievements in music. He was the leading organist of his day, and wherever he gave a concert the halls were crowded. He was soon to complete his third doctoral degree—in music. What was the answer he had arrived at that brought him such happiness? This is what he wrote.

It struck me as incomprehensible that I should be allowed to lead such a happy life, while I saw so many people around me wrestling with care and suffering. While at school I felt stirred when I caught a glimpse of the miserable home surroundings of some of my school fellows, and compared them with the ideal conditions in which we children lived in the parsonage at Günsbach. While in the University and enjoying the happiness of being able to study and even produce some results in science and art, I could not help thinking continually of others who were denied their happiness by their material circumstances or their health. Then one brilliant summer morning at Günsbach (1896) there came to me the thought that I must not accept this happiness as a matter of course, but must give something in return for it. Proceeding to think the matter out at once with calm deliberation, while the birds were singing outside, I settled with myself before I got up, that I would give myself to my science and art without abandon until I was 30 years old and this would enable me from that time onward to devote myself to the service of humanity. This for me was what Jesus was saying when he said, 'Whoever would save his life shall lose it and whosoever shall lose his life for my sake and the gospel's shall find it.'

Schweitzer tried, at first, to realize his goal by working with orphans or rehabilitating tramps and newly released prisoners, but after short experiments with these forms of service he was not satisfied. Then came a call to serve as a medical missionary in a remote jungle area in equitorial Africa. This was what he decided to do.

At thirty years of age he began his medical studies—a thorough preparation that was to take ten years. Then for more than forty years, he gave himself to the people of Africa, returning to Europe from time to time to play the organ in great cathedrals, thus earning the money to build his hospital, to heal the wounds and cure the sickness of those who needed him most. In losing his life he found it, not only for himself but he brought life to many others.

That may be true for such a man as Schweitzer, but what of ordinary folk like you and me?

When James B. Conant was president of Harvard he had a model of a turtle on his desk. This seemed strange until one read the inscription: "Consider the turtle. He makes progress only when he sticks his neck out." No one can live a life dedicated to God if he hides in his own shell. Progress is made by those who stick their necks out.

And speaking of turtles, you recall the story of the tortoise and the hare. They were to run a race, and the hare took a flying leap and was out of sight before the tortoise passed the first rock. But the hare got hungry and after a good meal he fell asleep. By the time he woke up, the slow tortoise had crossed the finish line.

Once we were like the hare in our speed and mobility. We were able to jump and run and scamper. Now we are more like the tortoise. Our pace is slower, our movements somewhat cumbersome. But with patience we run the race that is set before us, and we are prepared to lose some of the glamorous fringe benefits of life in order to find life's deeper meaning. It may cost us something to stick our necks out but when we do, we come to grips with life where it counts most. To do otherwise would be to stand holding selfishly to our racket, denying ourselves and others the benefits that come when we give something of ourselves to others.

The great poet Edwin Markham put this in memorable language in his poem, "Live and Help Live."

> Live and let live was the call of the old,
>   The call of the world when the world was cold,
> The call of men when they pulled apart,
>   The call of the race with a chill on its heart.
> But live and help live is the cry of the new,
>   The cry of the world with the dream shining through,
> The cry of the brother-world rising to birth,
>   The cry of the Christ for a comrade-like earth.

ONE STEP AT A TIME

Psalm 23

I first met her when I went back to India during World War II. Stella Ebersole had a face that radiated the joy of living. Her eyes were sparklingly alert, and the lines of her face made each part of it into a smile, including the twinkle of her eyes. She even had a merry voice and a chuckle along with her witty comments. Only then did I hear a bit about the long trek she had made from Burma that had almost cost her her life.

She had been in Burma as a missionary for a number of years. She was completely absorbed in her work as an evangelist and teacher. Then as the Japanese came closer and closer to her city, both the Burmese and foreigners were urged to pack up and leave. She was past middle age, small of stature, and had never been athletic or physically robust.

There was no time for delay. Quickly she put into a pack the clothing, medicines, and food she would herself have to carry the hundreds of uncharted miles through the dense rain-forests that separated Burma from India. Though she began the trek without a companion, she soon discovered that hundreds were in flight. It was not long before she began to pass those who because of age or sickness or fear could go no further. The rains descended, making the trail miserable. Shelters, such as they were, were few and always over-crowded. When she was almost at the end of her strength, she looked ahead and through the monsoon clouds saw the line of mountains she would have to cross. Up and up she climbed until she was completely exhausted. Often she did not think she would be able to start again the next day. It was then she learned an important lesson. Somehow there was strength enough to take the next step and sure enough, when night came, she had made some progress—not as much as the ones who were younger or who had lighter loads or better shoes, but she survived because she took one step at a time.

The Christian is one who is poised in a forward posture, ready to use the resources of God to move forward. The sheer demands of life weigh so heavily on some, they are almost paralyzed. An operation, a tragic loss, the arthritic pain in the joints, the unexplained loneliness within the same four walls day by day, the feeling of insecurity and discomfort. Whatever it is that forms a mountain wall that shuts us from freedom and robs us of the hoped-for years of comfort we had dreamed of, may turn us into frightened souls, unless we resolve to confront them one step at a time.

How remarkable that when we draw on the strength God has given us in body, mind, and spirit, we not only manage to endure, we may become persons of radiant strength and inspiration to others. That was what I found in Stella Ebersole. She didn't depend on her own strength but in the strength God had given her and in that strength she took one step at a time. In spite of drenched trails through tiger-infested jungles and though she had to climb mountains with a heavy pack on her back, she met the demands of each day. She not only survived, she conquered in the strength God had given her.

Joseph H. Gilmore's great hymn, "He Leadeth Me," has helped a multitude of afflicted and weary persons take those steps forward.

> He leadeth me: O blessed thought!
> O words with heavenly comfort frought.
> Whate'er I do, Where'er I be,
> Still 'tis God's hand that leadeth me.
>
> Sometimes 'mid scenes of deepest gloom,
> Sometimes where Eden's bowers bloom,
> By waters still, o'er troubled sea,
> Still 'tis His hand that leadeth me.
>
> Lord, I would place my hand in Thine,
> Nor ever murmur nor repine;
> Content, whatever lot I see,
> Since 'tis my God that leadeth me.
>
> And when my task on earth is done,
> When, by Thy grace, the victory's won,
> E'en death's cold wave I will not flee,
> Since God thro' Jordon leadeth me.

THE SECRET OF THE ORDINARY

Matthew 25:20-23

On one of my trips to India I passed through Johannesburg, South Africa. I didn't get out of the train and go to those rich diamond-mines that make that part of the world so famous, but the other day I read a story that made me remember that trip through South Africa.

In the story, the manager of one of the mines was said to have formed the habit of leaving his desk at noon to walk through one of the diggings. On a day he would never forget, as he walked along he saw a sparkle of light. He reached down for what he thought was probably a carelessly thrown piece of a bottle. On closer examination he discovered that it was a large and beautiful diamond, in fact, the largest ever found in the mine. He was immediately faced with a problem. How could this priceless gem be transported from South Africa to London so it could be processed and sold? He gave the matter much thought, and then decided on a solution he believed to be best.

Four men were given a small square package to carry under guard throughout the long journey. They had to walk sixty miles through the jungle before they would reach the railway. Two stayed on guard at all times day and night while the others rested. At the railway, a special car had been provided to carry only the four of them with their parcel to the seaport. Before they boarded the ship they paid a high price to have a specially built safe welded to the ship's hull where they kept the box under guard at all times. When they arrived in England, a special train was waiting under heavy police guard, to take them to London. There they delivered the box safely.

The diamond cutters were waiting for the gem; they crowded around, each hoping to be the first to see the beautiful stone. At last the box was opened, and much to their surprise and complete astonishment all that was in the box was a small piece of black coal. Where was the diamond? What had become of it? Then they heard the rest of the story.

The wise manager back in South Africa had wrapped the diamond in ordinary brown paper and cotton packing. He had put it in an ordinary small box and did it up as an ordinary parcel and sent it through the mail as he would any other parcel. Not even the post office had been aware what that ordinary parcel contained. The parcel had made the trip over thousands of miles just like any other piece of mail. It had received no special attention and had arrived safely at its destination. The manager was asked, "Why did you do it that way?" He then told them that the postal system had been trustworthy through the years, had handled small things safely, and if it could handle small things with honesty and pride, it could be trusted with great things.

You have probably already thought of some of the things we could learn from this incident. First, we grow in character, not so much in the manner we handle the big things of life—the major opportunities—as the way we handle little, everyday relationships and affairs. After we have learned to handle small things well, then we can meet moments of great stress equally as well. As we develop ways to be friendly, helpful, concerned, and compassionate, no emergency will find us unprepared.

Secondly, this story helps us see how one of Jesus' teachings works out in actual life. In Matthew 25:20-23, he told his disciples that if they were faithful in little things, they would be given much and they would be able to share that with others.

Thirdly, we also see that often it is not the most beautiful nor the most expensive that has the greatest value in life. It must have cost what would be for most of us a fortune to send that bit of coal guarded as it was from South Africa to London. Spending all that money didn't add anything to the real worth of the lump of coal. It isn't what is put on the outside but what is on the inside that gives a thing its real value.

More often than not the real gems of life are found in the ordinary. I hope that is so. Your worth and mine will not be judged by our finery or grandeur but by our ability to use the ordinary to do extraordinary things. Jesus saw the significance of that. He didn't go into the Temple and choose the High Priest or into the Forum and call the Roman Governor and give them the task of setting free the Kingdom of God on earth. Rather, he entrusted the eternal Gospel of Love to ordinary men and women. Peter and Andrew were fishermen. Matthew was a tax-collector, the others were boys from the countryside. It was said that he looked out on the multitudes—the common people—and was moved with compassion for they were as sheep without a shepherd. He was surrounded by ordinary men and women and these were they who later turned the world upside down.

97

This is what fills life so full of possibilities for each one of us. We are ordinary, then God blesses us and uses us to add sparkle and delight and spiritual joy to others. Our ordinary is transformed until life is filled with vast riches of character and spiritual experiences. We have seen it happen to others and it can happen in us. Life becomes exciting when God helps us transform our ordinary into the extraordinary.

A BETTER POINT OF VIEW

Colossians 1:3-14; Isaiah 55:6-9,12,13

We eagerly look forward to quiet moments of worship such as these when we expect something to happen as we wait in God's presence. We free ourselves from ordinary thoughts and deeds so we can get a clearer perspective of the whole of life—its problems and tensions—its joys and sorrows—and seek to know the many ways God is opening up our lives for good. The Apostle Paul urged people to worship, "that you might be filled with all spiritual wisdom and understanding." (Colossians 1:9b) Phillips, in an early translation of the passage used slightly different words: we worship to see things "from God's point of view."

The great prophet, Isaiah, eagerly turned to God as he tried to find answers to what troubled and plagued him and others and he heard God say,

As the heavens are higher than the earth, so are my ways higher than your ways, and my thoughts than your thoughts. ... My word shall not return to me empty, but it shall accomplish that which I purpose, and prosper in the things for which I sent it. For you shall go out in joy and be led forth in peace. (Isaiah 55:9, 11f.)

That changed things for Isaiah. We, too, can use our moments of meditation to look freshly at our lives from God's point of view and be lifted above our limited understanding.

Worship is a time when we take a fresh look at ourselves. Each one meets life a bit differently. The smiles on our faces may reflect inner joy and happiness, and we may be bubbling over because of good things that have happened. But those smiles may be our brave way of facing today's world when it has not been friendly and we have a heavy burden on our heart. Few people go through a week without moments of discouragement, loneliness, or fear, to say nothing of physical pain. In such times we are inclined to say that things are really bad and we begin to lose hope.

Paul knew how important it is not to lose heart, "that we might be filled with all spiritual wisdom and understanding." We may be certain, God is trying to speak to our needs. Meditation is a time when we become receptive and more clearly see our lives from God's point of view. God helps us see life in its grander design, above our limited view, our partial understanding. We need that every day of our lives.

Second, in meditation we gain a better understanding of others. Napoleon, we are told, after a victory that lost him thousands of ordinary soldiers, brushed it aside, saying, "We lost no one important."

In contrast, you remember the hymn, "There were ninety and nine that safely lay in the shelter of the fold, but one was out on the hills away. ..." The Good Shepherd went out to find the one that was lost. Meditation helps us discover the infinite worth of every person when we begin to see life from God's point of view. All are of equal value in his sight. We have his word for it.

Our attitude toward others either lifts or lowers our warm response to them and our ability to contribute to their welfare. We have a tendency, when we do not know them, to classify them as blacks, browns, reds, whites, good, bad, kind, cruel, or just unimportant. We could hardly get a proper attitude toward New Yorkers if we viewed them only from the top of the Empire State Building. We would not want God to hold us at arm's length but to draw us into the sheepfold of his compassion and understanding. As we meditate and pray for other people, for individuals and nations both near and far, we begin to see them from God's point of view. Our world is suddenly filled with people who have meaning for our lives and our hearts are stretched and our faith strengthened as we share God's point of view.

God's point of view also enters into our judgement and helps us put a different value on what is important and what constitutes success. Jesus was not impressed by status. When he called men and women to be his disciples, he chose such men as Simon Peter, a fisherman;

Matthew, a tax-collector; and among the others there were none of social or business importance. It was to such as these he told the parables of the Kingdom of God. The Kingdom is like a mustard seed, the smallest of seeds, but it utilizes its potential and becomes a tree to give shelter to the birds. The Kingdom is like yeast, too small to be seen, but when put in dough, it multiplies until the whole loaf is permeated with yeast; it becomes the bread of life. Jesus did not measure others by their self-importance but according to the way they permitted God to enlarge and energize their lives.

Within a century after the time of Jesus, Christianity had spread over much of the Roman world. At the Colosseum, in Rome, there were great spectacles, to give pleasure to the Emperor. Christians were there. Some were made to fight lions and were torn apart. Others were smeared with pitch and hung on crosses, then lit to form living torches to light the arena. Christians were the small, insignificant ones of the Empire. Yet it was "the blood of the martyrs that became the seed of the church." Their terrible trials, that at the time must have seemed difficult to understand, were turned into a powerful force for good. Ours is a victorious faith; the secret of it is seen in our individual and group response to God, even as our faith is fortified and strengthened in worship and meditation.

Paul was right. In worship we expect much. We wait before God to be filled with "all wisdom and understanding," and when this happens, as Paul says, God delivers us "from the dominion of darkness and transforms us to the kingdom of his beloved Son in whom we have redemption."

How does God turn a meditation into a redemptive experience? When we look at our tormenting problems from God's point of view, with his help they can add to our understanding, add to our sympathetic outreach and compassion and become in us vibrant spiritual powers that may well become doorways of faith for others. This has been my personal experience. What at first seemed to crush me, was gradually changed through worship and meditation, so I emerged with my faith strengthened and my understanding clarified. I give thanks for those moments when I could look at life anew from God's point of view.

God not only knows the depth of human anguish, for he lost a Son on a cruel cross, but he touches every life to fill us with spiritual wisdom and understanding and delivers us "from the dominion of darkness and transforms us to the kingdom of his beloved Son in whom we have redemption." That lets us see life from a better point of view.

LIVING WITH OURSELVES

Psalm 8:3-9, 17, 18

Dr. Norman Vincent Peale, a famous minister in New York, reminds us that we all have to learn to live with ourselves. Whether we are young or old, black or white, brown or yellow, or whether we are astronauts flying through space or someone lying prone in a nursing home, all of us have to live with ourselves; we have to do it twenty-four hours a day, seven days a week, every week of the year.

It might seem then, that since everyone must do this, most people would learn how to do it well. But in fact some are miserable and tend to make everyone else miserable around them. Others give the impression they are martyrs, enduring and suffering through one tragedy after another. But there are a glorious company of healthy and stimulating men and women who seem to be having the time of their lives, not because everything is going their way or they live on a bed of roses, but because they have developed an attitude toward life that makes the difference. They sift out life's miseries and catch hold of the glories of their past and present and release life's juices that radiate all through their loving, caring, soul-inspiring personalities.

What makes the difference? It begins with what they think of themselves. There is a tendency among some who are older to look on themselves as worn-out relics of what they once were. Well, let us face it, we are likely not as agile as we once were. No doubt there were some who lived at the time of the psalmist who had a rather low view of themselves, but the psalmist thought differently.

> What is man that thou art mindful of him,
> And the son of man that thou dost care for him?
> Yet thou hast made him little lower than God,
> And dost crown him with glory and honor.

In the book of Genesis we are told that God made us in his own image; and the psalmist here finds that that image—God's image, is indeed stamped on us.

These words should make us aware of our dignity and worth. We are the very crown of creation. You may say, "That was once true when I was in my prime, but now my world has changed; my active years have passed; I am captive to a body that is not strong." In our later years it is more difficult to travel and we may find it difficult to participate in the many activities that once gave us such delight, but

101

the loss of these external engagements do not necessarily diminish our dignity and worth. There are God-given ways to adjust to changes that are certain to come.

1. The psalmist didn't say that only those who are young or middle-aged are a little lower than God. Our dignity is not a time capsule. This dignity is ours because we are the creation of God; and this is true no matter what our age or condition. We must not let the aging process rob us of the very god-likeness that is ours for "In him we live and move and have our being." (Acts 17:28) This is not true for only those who are young or who live independently or who can still play golf. Our worth does not depend on the special creams that we use to keep our skin looking young, nor on the slim and trim diets available in twenty-four weeks of torturous living. The evidences of being a little lower than God show through when we claim the dignity and human potential that is ours as children of God.

A most important secret is to draw on God's power so that his glory continues to fill our lives; when that happens we have within us the strength and courage and joy for even the most trying moments we may ever know. When we pause to reflect, we must admit that among the most beautiful, vibrant personalities we have known are some who have been clothed in broken bodies. Two men were born on the same day, February 12, 1809. One lived in England, the other in America, but they had this in common. Both grew up under handicaps. Charles Darwin looked back on his life and said, "If I had not been so great an invalid, I would not have done so much work as I accomplished." His handicap kept him at his scientific experiments. The other man born on that day was Abraham Lincoln. He was raised in poverty and lacked a formal education, yet he wrote one of the finest phrases in the human language: "With malice toward none; with charity toward all. ..." It is not what our circumstances are, but whether we permit what happens to us to drain off our human dignity that makes the difference.

2. If we accept this high regard of ourselves, that we are a little lower than God, then we had better stop shutting our lives up in small snug compartments and open them to the great things of God. We begin this when we break away from bondage to familiar routines and surroundings and welcome new experiences. We need to drink in fresh strength through physical and mental exercise. Our bodies need nutritious food; this may call for new eating habits and a development of new tastes. We must learn ways to become flexible. We are told that the largest land animals that ever lived, the

dinosaurs, disappeared from off the earth because they never learned how to be flexible. They failed to adapt to changes in climate, food, and terrain, or a combination of these. We will need to change those habits that prove contrary to our highest potential, and this happens when we open up our lives to the great things of God. Every one of us has built right into his or her life those vital powers such as love, compassion, inner peace, and other powers that we have hardly begun to use. To quote Dr. Peale again, "You are greater than you think, and in the name of Jesus Christ, your savior, you can become the human being God intended you to be."

3. Let Dr. Peale end with another affirmation. "You are greater than anything that will ever happen to you. With God's help and guidance you can handle anything that will ever happen to you. Nothing in this world can ever defeat you, if you constantly reaffirm to yourself, 'I have been given dominion by God, my Father. I have glory and honor from Almighty God Himself.'"

When we accept ourselves as being little lower than God, when we "live and move and have our being" in him, we begin to show the dignity and worth of the family of God, no matter what our age or what walls have closed in around us.

COMING TO GRIPS WITH LIFE AND DEATH
Matthew 26:36-45

There has always been a deep affection between my mother and me. During much of her life she passed through periods of sickness, and she seemed to depend on me in a special way to help in various ways about the house. But a time came when I was half way around the world as a missionary, and we were separated for periods of five or six years at a time. During our furloughs in America, Mother lived with us as much of the time as possible. She wrote, after I returned to India following my first furlough, and I still have the letter, "More than anything else, I wish that you could be here with me now." Then she added, "No, that is not what I really want. I wish that you will always do right, wherever you are." What a wonderful wish for a mother to make to her son.

103

On a later furlough, she was with us until just before we left again for India. Then the day came that I had to put her on a bus so she could return to be with my sister. The bus was about to leave when she reached for my hand and said, "James, I'm afraid. I'm afraid to die. I'm afraid of the future." It was the first she had ever expressed fear, for she had always been a very religious person. I had no time to respond, for only a moment later the bus pulled out. I felt helpless to comfort or reassure her. It was five years before I saw her again. We had exchanged many letters and by then her fear was gone. She greeted me with the assurance, "I'm no more afraid."

When we come to grips with the meaning of life, or a change occurs in our physical strength, or a financial or social problem arises, and especially when we permit the mystery of death to surmount our certainties about the future, we are somewhat like Jesus was in the Garden of Gethsemane. You remember the people had welcomed him into Jerusalem, waving palm branches, laying their cloaks on the road, and throwing flowers on the way. Then his enemies moved in; and he knew they were out to get him, so he went out of the city to the little garden. Leaving even his closest friends some distance, he fell on his knees and poured out his heart to God. Even Jesus found these problems more than he could handle by himself. He prayed so fervently, we are told, that it was as if there were great drops of blood on his forehead. "If it be your will—let this cup pass, nevertheless, not my will, but thine be done." He had asked his closest friends to watch and pray with him one hour, but when he went to them he found them sleeping.

More than likely we will have to face our moments of agony very much alone. There is only so much others, even our dearest relatives or friends, can do to help at such times. We would remember Jesus in the garden and recall how, almost at once after he had said, "Not my will but thine," he seemed to find peace and assurance; and he arose in strength able to face even the terrible cross. When we make this our prayer, when we accept God's will, there comes a calm and radiance in our lives; peace is certain to follow.

This came to my mother. I was with her as often as possible during the last furlough before she died. She could not live with us then, for she had had a stroke and needed the care of a nursing home. They were exceedingly kind to her. Her mind was alert and I was delighted to spend even a few moments with her. I was forever criss-crossing the State, almost constantly speaking in churches, schools, or other gatherings.

On my last visit I had driven two hundred miles to have an hour with her late in the afternoon before going to a dinner meeting in a near-by town. When I left she took my hand and said, "God bless you." She had never said those words in just that way. Later, I was told that when my sister stopped only a few minutes after I had left, Mother was in a coma; the next night she was gone. She had come to grips with life. Her Gethsemane had prepared her to say, "I'm not afraid."

Coming to grips with life and death involve many experiences that can be rewarding. For my mother it meant overcoming the fear of death. In my conversations with her I found she at last accepted the fact that death is a part of life. Isaiah, the prophet, wrote, "All flesh is grass and all its beauty is like the flower of the field. The grass withers, the flowers fades when the breath of the Lord blows upon it; surely the people is grass." That may be true of our bodies as they become old, but like Isaiah, Mother had discovered a greater truth and Isaiah had a further word, "The grass withers, the flower fades, but the word of the Lord endures forever." Mother's faith went even further for it included the resurrection of Jesus and the affirmation that the spiritual quality of life is eternal.

Such faith embodies mysteries that we cannot fully understand. The spirit-filled saints who wrote the scriptures probed into life after death. Their answers are not fully satisfying but out of what has been written, I detect those certainties that comforted Mother and made it possible for her to say, "I am not afraid."

She was reassured by Isaiah's words that "the word of the Lord endures forever." This is another way of affirming God's steadfast love, a love that surrounds us eternally and encompasses both life and death. Our bodies may change, but God's love is steadfast, unchanging, true. It does not change. And this leads to a further affirmation. Death is not a miracle, suddenly making us something we have not been before. Death is a doorway through which our spirits pass, for our spirits are eternal. Our bodies are as grass. They wither. "Dust thou art, to dust returneth," but, as the poet said, that was "not spoken of the soul."

Mother felt a joy and peace in her awareness of her oneness with God. She had enjoyed a spirit-filled life. Her faith had been her delight long after her body lay paralyzed. She had already experienced a certain boundlessness of spirit beyond the limitations of physical frailty, as she lay hardly able to move, so she was certain that, when her body dropped away, there would be a tomorrow for her spirit. Because she had learned she could trust God during all the days of her life, now, as she was passing through the door of death, she gloried in being able to trust his unchanging love, for his ways and his words are eternal.

Truly, she was no longer afraid; nor have I been on numerous occasions, in storms or submarine attacks on the high seas, in streets aflame with rioting and fanatical violence in distant cities, or lying desperately ill and uncertain of physical survival. How often I felt welling up within me a sure confidence of God's steadfast love and it removed all fear of death. I felt underneath the everlasting arms. Both Mother and I, as our faith matured, were without fear. No one can know exactly what it will be like when our lives on earth are past, but we know God, and we can trust the future to him as we have the past.

EVERYONE NEEDS COMFORT

II Corinthians 1:3-7, Luke 23:39-43

We never outgrow the basic human need for comfort, a comfort such as we knew as little children when our mothers gathered us in their arms and kissed away our tears. This deep need never goes away, no matter how old we become and we feel it most strongly in moments of crisis.

I stood at the bedside of a woman only a few days ago. That mother was in anguish, not because of her own serious illness from which she has since died, but because her son had suffered a stroke and his life was in danger. As a loving mother, she asked, "Won't you pray for my son. Ask God to give him strength." She needed comfort.

Such moments, when you or I are in the presence of those who experience anguish, you have felt, as I have, how eagerly you would like to cradle them to your breast and hold them lovingly so you could bring comfort to them.

It was to such people that St. Paul wrote his letter (to the Corinthians) and he spoke of God as a "God of all comfort." All through that letter Paul catalogues one experience after another in which people reached out for God's comfort. In a later chapter he writes of his own chilling moments of suffering, when his spirit was almost broken with anguish, and had it not been for his Christian faith, he would not have endured. God comforted him.

Put yourself in Paul's place, if you will, and try to imagine not only how he suffered physically, but what must have gone through his mind while he endured these terrible experiences. "Five times I received forty lashes save one, three times beaten with rods, once stoned, three times shipwrecked, a night and a day I have been adrift at sea; on frequent journeys, in danger in the city, danger in the wilderness. ... through many sleepless nights, in hunger and thirst, often without food, in cold and exposure. ..." You see, he was speaking from experience, when he called God a God of all comfort. "Blessed be the God and Father of our Lord Jesus Christ, the Father of mercies and God of all comfort, who comforts us in all our afflictions so that we may be able to comfort those who are in affliction with the comfort we ourselves are comforted by God."

Paul said, God comforts us so that we can extend such comfort to others. Jesus looked upon this as a very important part of his ministry. In his very first sermon he expressed this longing to bring comfort. "The Spirit of the Lord is upon me, because he has anointed me to preach good news to the poor. He has sent me to proclaim release to the captives and recovering of sight to the blind, to set at liberty those who are oppressed, to proclaim the acceptable year of the Lord." (Luke 4:18)

Some of us when we accept divine forgiveness experience God's comfort at life's deepest level. I know of no more powerful illustration of this than I found in a film made some years ago to tell the story of John Wesley. One scene showed how a tormented young boy was comforted when he received God's forgiveness. While Wesley was a student at Oxford, he went as often as he could to work among prisoners at Ludgate jail. When convicts were put in carts to be carried to the gallows, Wesley would ride with them and comfort them. On one occasion, a youth became terrified as he thought of eternal punishment. Then Wesley told how Jesus, during the crucifixion, had offered God's pardon to a thief who hung on a near-by cross, and how that thief had been comforted when Jesus said, "Today, you will be with me in Paradise." Wesley assured the young prisoner that God would hear his prayer for forgiveness, because God is eager to forgive a penitent child. As the prisoner listened, he asked for God's pardon, and before they reached the place of execution, he was forgiven. His face lit up as he felt comfort and peace; God's comfort, such as we too, can know when our sins are forgiven.

When Paul stressed that God comforts us so we can comfort those in affliction, he was striking on a very significant fact of life. Often our anguish and sorrow continue and our misery deepens until something happens to make us forget ourselves, because we are called on to bring comfort to others.

The story is told of Narcissa Whitman, the first white woman to cross the Rockies back at the time settlers were opening up the West. She and her husband had gone into the wilderness and there they built their cabin. Then one day she watched helplessly as her first born was carried beyond her reach into deep waters of the river and drowned. In the weeks that followed, nothing could comfort her. Day after day she sat mournful and was overcome with grief. The season changed, the snows came and caught the Donner party in what is now known as Donner Pass in the high Sierras. Most of the party died of starvation, but one day eleven orphans, survivors of that tragedy, stood before the Whitman cabin—hungry, homeless, lost. Narcissa Whitman's heart was touched. Now she had work to do. She must bring comfort to children who had lost their parents and who had endured such terrible suffering. She welcomed them into her home and heart. She made them her children. She not only comforted them but her own heart was comforted. Paul was right, God comforts us so we are able to comfort those in affliction.

Everyone needs comfort: the sinner, the saint, youth, age. We are told of the good St. Francis of Assisi, who toward the end of his life was in constant pain so he could not sleep at night and every moment of the day he suffered physical torment. He sought comfort. As he turned to God his mind went back to the beautiful valley of his childhood. He thought of the times he would lie in the fields looking up at the clouds and the sky. He began to think of the mysteries of fire, wind, flowing water, growing things; soon he realized he was surrounded with evidences of God and this comforted him. He found God everywhere and was filled with wonder and worship. Comfort flooded his mind and heart, and he put his thoughts into one of his beautiful hymns, "All Creatures Great and Small." The verses still bring comfort: the burning sun, the rushing wind, the clouds, the flowing water, the flowers and fruit, the men of tender heart. As he thought of these he forgot his agony. They comforted him, for as Paul said, "God is a God of all comfort."

Spiritual comfort in the deep recesses of our minds may be attached to vivid memories our of our childhood and youth. God can use them for our comfort when some of the more active avenues of comfort are closed.

Everyone needs comfort and God is eagerly waiting to extend just that form of comfort we need most, for "God is the God of all comfort."

INVITATION TO LIFE
Matthew 22:1-9

Many people have the idea that religion doesn't add excitement or happiness to life; rather, it throws something of a wet blanket over enjoyment and all else that might add luster to living. There must have been those who thought like that in Jesus' day, but that was not his idea of religion. The words joy, rejoice, and be glad were an important part of his vocabulary. He tried to lift people out of their traditional notions of religion. He invited them to become a company of merrymakers and spoke of them as members of the Kingdom of God or the Kingdom of Heaven. In one of his teachings he compared them to people who took part in a marriage feast. A marriage feast in those days was not just a sumptious supper in a near-by hotel; it was days of festivity, games, family reunion, feasting, and good fun for all—young and old alike. Jesus was telling them that faith in God leads to a joyful experience and should be satisfying and completely memorable; it should bring joy to all who share it.

In this story of the marriage feast (Matthew 22:1-9), Jesus told of some who had been invited but did not want to come. They just continued in their old ways. Others, when they were invited, took it as an insult and even did bodily harm to those who had delivered the invitations. But their refusal did not cancel things out, rather the king ordered his messengers to extend the invitation and admit all who would come; soon the halls were filled with joyous laughter.

What Jesus was saying was that just as you cannot enjoy a wedding feast unless you accept the invitation, so you cannot participate in joyous religious experiences as members of the Kingdom, unless you accept the invitation to share all that God is ready to give you and do for you. We miss out on much of the fun of life when we do not acknowledge that we live in God's world and must attune our lives accordingly. Only when we do so can we share the joy and happiness that comes when we accept the invitation to some of the things that make religion like a marriage feast. Such invitations come to us almost every day. Here are some of them.

1.   There is the invitation to be aware of the beauty and wonder of God's world. Some may not, because of physical limitations, be able to experience them directly, but even they can find delight when they meditate upon them. A poet has said that if only we fully understood a rose, we would know much about God. What gives color to such a flower? What causes it to open up so that even after it is put into a room it gives out its sweet perfume? Or we look into the sky and see the clouds changing shape, moving and lifting before the wind, opening up at times to give us rain. There on the horizon are trees bending in the breeze and nearby are the waters of a river opening into the bay.

On those days when life seems especially difficult, stop and think of the invitation to see the beauty and wonder of God's world. Instead of counting sheep in a long sleepless night, list some of those beauties and recall one in every detail. Accept the invitation to find beauty in God's world and let your heart be filled with wonder, mystery, and spiritual joy.

2.   There are invitations to share the thoughts of great souls through reading. The story is told of a man who stood in a library looking out on a rainy day. He was heard to say, "What on earth can a man do on a day like this?" The walls of the library were lined with books and those books were filled with the wisdom of the ages. There was mirth, there were the visions of great men; words waiting to be read that would excite his mind and lift his spirit.

You may find it hard to read. The invitation then may come in a different form. Recall poems you have learned in school or great thoughts you have heard or read. There may be favorite passages of scripture, the Psalms, or the words of Jesus. Enjoy the wedding feast of literature and know such joy and excitement in the company of great minds of the past.

This surely would include the invitation to think creatively and positively, not letting evil or selfish thoughts fill your mind. Build pyramids of kind, good, and compassionate thoughts. God invites you to think his thoughts after him. What an up-lift comes as we do this.

3. There is the invitation to hold communion with God—to feel God's love surrounding you. When you do this you will turn off your contrary or complaining spirit and let God's love fill your life. When this happens those negative, evil, and thankless feelings will give way to positive, helpful, gracious thoughts.

In Virginia, there is a break in the trees along the Appalachian Trail up on Big Walker Mountain. You pause and look down on a lush green valley, and your eyes are lifted to the mountain climbing into the sky across the valley. It is majestic. It is awe inspiring. Its breathtaking beauty lifts your soul.

We need a break in the skyline of our day—moments of prayer and meditation, when God lifts us above our low and self-centered concerns and gives us a spirit-filled view of his plan for our lives. That invitation to hold communion with God comes every day.

4. The most important invitation of all may be to respond to human need near-by. Jesus told of Dives and Lazarus. (Luke 16:19ff.) Dives was a hard-hearted, selfish, rich man who feasted on the best food while Lazarus starved outside his door. The tragedy was that Dives passed him every day and never saw him.

We could be like Dives. We may not be rich, but we can become so absorbed in ourselves, so sorry for ourselves, so eager to get the best of every situation that we do not see the need around us. It is likely true that we really do not live until we bring delight and joy to someone else. It makes us different when we are aware of those who are sick or lonely or who may be reaching out, waiting for a kind word or gesture. The invitation to respond in outgoing kindness to others makes us rejoice and be glad.

Religion then is no drab, soul pinching, joyless, hum-drum existence. It is a festival of the soul. Our religion should do these things for us, and more. Unless and until our faith serves to fill life full of radiant joy, we have not fully accepted the invitation to the marriage feast. But that invitation is waiting for us today and we can go in with the others and fill the hall with joyous laughter.

A LOOK AT THE EVIDENCE

Luke 7:36 ff., Mark 10:46-52

Roy H. Stetler wrote in a book of devotions about an imaginary trip he took to Jerusalem to find evidences of Jesus and what he wrote set me thinking. What evidences of Jesus do we have that are authentic? What Mr. Stetler wrote may help you discover something new about Jesus.

When he got to Jerusalem he began right away to look for evidences of Jesus. He engaged a guide to show him the place of the crucifixion. There is still a formation in the rock that looks like a skull, and so is called, "The place of the skull." And not far away is a cemetery known as the "Potters Field," which is the burial place for criminals and drifters who die without a family to bury them. Tradition has it that it was bought with the thirty pieces of silver Judas received for turning Jesus over to the authorities. Not until Judas had seen Jesus led away to be crucified did he realize what a terrible thing he had done. It was too late then to give the silver back and we are told it paid for the Potters Field.

Then the guide took him to a gift shop; and at once the shopkeeper tried to interest him in various relics. He opened up a secret place and brought out some twisted branches covered with thorns. "These," he said, "were part of the crown they put on Jesus' head." There was a longer branch which he said was the reed they put in Jesus' hands before they mocked him and pretended he was their king. "These," said the shopkeeper, "are not for sale, but here are fragments of wood," and he uncovered some, "that are part of the cross, and you can buy one of them." Mr. Stetler was anxious to have something from the crucifixion, so he bought a small piece of wood. Then he asked, "Don't you have one of the nails?" The guide was quick to offer, "They don't have any here, but they have some across the street." So they crossed to the other shop and at last Mr. Stetler held one of the nails in his hand, but he was not satisfied. The nail was not for sale, and in any case, there was no blood on it. Seeing his disappointment, the guide led him out of the shop to the tomb. There Mr. Stetler picked up some flakes of rock, for he thought they might just possibly be from the rock that was rolled away that first Easter morning.

Returning to his hotel Mr. Stetler began to think. Were the thorns, the wood, the nails, the rocks the real evidence of the crucifixion? He knew they had sentimental value for some, but he asked himself whether one could find real evidence about Jesus or about God in such things. Could one come to know Jesus as the "Light of the World," by looking at such relics? Or does real evidence lie elsewhere?

As I say, Mr. Stetler's imaginary visit to Jerusalem set me thinking. Why does Jesus seem real to me? I have never had much interest in relics. Surely there must be more authentic evidence that has real meaning for us. I believe Mr. Stetler was right to question in his own mind whether this was what he wanted to find.

We have to look elsewhere; and when we do we find it in abundance. What a difference Jesus made in human experience when men and women have responded to the words, "Behold I stand at the door and knock, if any man will open I will come in and eat with him and he with me." (Revelation 3:20) This begins to open up real evidence. People in almost every nation of the world are consciously aware of the living presence of Jesus in moments of their need and during prayerful meditation. And an experience of the presence of Jesus speaks so loud they cannot hear what the thorns and wood and rocks have to say. As I thought of this I began to discover this deeper kind of evidence throughout the records of Jesus.

What must it have been like for blind Bartimaeus, who sat along the road outside Jericho? He had a completely authentic evidence of Jesus when Jesus touched his eyes, and the face of Jesus came into focus as his eyes responded to the light. What an evidence that must have been.

What of the children? It was probably true in Jesus' day as it is in ours that children were to be seen and not heard. What an evidence of God's love for those parents when Jesus told his disciples not to send the children away—when he took up a little child and blessed it. What did it mean to that child, and to his parents, when Jesus put him in the circle of Rabbis, Elders, and parents and said, "Unless you become as little children, you cannot enter the Kingdom of Heaven." That would be better evidence than blood on a rusty nail.

Or the woman who came to anoint Jesus in the home of a Pharisee. She was a "woman of the streets,"—a sinner in the sight of all those present, and she anointed Jesus' feet and kissed them before wiping them with her hair. Jesus said that she had sinned much and had been forgiven much, so the costly ointment showed the measure of her gratitude for God's merciful forgiveness. After this act of faith,

Jesus told her to go in peace. What poor evidence is a thorn or a rock compared to the transformation that came to this woman? Tradition identifies her with Mary Magdalene, who became a loyal follower and was with the mother of Jesus at the crucifixion.

Here was evidence that touched my heart. It was evidence in living tissue, but it was still outward, for it was what had happened to others. What evidence did I find in my own experience?

Then my mind jumped to the first time I was asked to tell what Jesus meant to me. I probably struggled for words then, for even now I cannot find an adequate language. But what a difference he has made in my life. I still have my problems. I struggle with selfishness and jealousy. I can be stubborn, even hot-tempered, and at times my mind and my eyes depart from the good and are inclined to evil. When I am tormented in these ways, I feel evidence of Jesus very deep within my soul. How different I would be without him. I almost shudder at times when I think what I might have done in some situations had I not been held steady in moments of temptation. I have been aware of a presence that does not let me be satisfied with an evil mind or a sinful act. In moments of decision he is there to guide me. What is pleasing to him is not only best for me but good for others. This, too, is evidence.

These authentic evidences in human experience weigh more than pieces of wood or nails or stone. He continues to move among men and women generation after generation. There may not have been any blood on the nail in the shop in Jerusalem, but these evidences are more profound. He continues to give shape to human life. You will want to look at such evidence yourself. It will make a difference in your life, too.

MORE THAN OUR OWN STRENGTH
II Timothy 1:6f, Philippians 4:13

Have you ever felt too tired or too sick or too weak to do the simplest things you are expected to do? I have. My sister once responded to my father in a jesting way. He had just asked her to do something, and she really didn't have a good excuse, but she didn't feel like doing it, so wittingly she remarked, "Oh, do it yourself. I believe in wearing out the oldest thing first," and then, of course, she did what she was asked to do.

Well, we all feel at times like saying, "Let someone else do it." But for our own good and to help make the world go round, and so we can all live together happily, we can't let someone else do our thing. We have to act ourselves, even if it is only speaking a cheerful word, or doing the little necessary things of life we can do. Even these, sometimes, seem almost too much for us.

The fact is, there isn't anyone in the whole world who is strong enough or great enough or wise enough to depend entirely on his own strength. The President of the United States—good, wise, powerful—falls flat on his face when he depends entirely on himself, and this is true of all of us. We are not sufficiently endowed with the wisdom to function properly when we leave God out. Whenever we try, and we are just stubborn enough to try, we fail. Fortunately we do not have to depend on our own strength. We, like Paul the Apostle, can draw on spiritual resources and with him say, "I can do all things through Christ who strengthens me."

When Paul was in prison, some of the people who should have been able to handle their own problems wrote and told him their troubles. In his reply he wrote, "I remind you to rekindle the gift of God that is within you. ... For God did not give us a spirit of weakness (timidity), but a spirit of power and love and self control."

My cousin had a strange fever when she was a girl of 12. It made her a cripple, and for 65 years Alice has been on crutches or in a wheel chair. When I visited her last she had just passed through a period of sickness, and to add to her discomfort the person who shared her room proved very inconsiderate, and there were tensions between them. This was almost more than she could bear, and I saw her at a time when her spirits were low and her faith faltered. She said, "All these years I have been supported by my faith. Sometimes

115

the pain is almost more than I can bear. Sometimes my faith grows weak and I almost lose hold of God." She asked, "What can I do? Can you help me?"

I have always loved Alice for she is a dear person. I know that she has suffered terribly. I do not know why she has suffered, but I could not help telling her what an inspiration she has been to me. Sometimes as a missionary, I became discouraged. Sometimes in the heat, fighting off mosquitoes, or lying in a hospital terribly sick with malaria or diarrhea or pneumonia, more than my physical strength was tested. Then I would think of Alice. During the years that I have known her she has shown a strong faith. I had only to pause a moment and I could recall her merry laughter, as she made her way across a room on her crutches. I also knew that she never lost an opportunity to help someone in need. She had a cheerful word for everyone. There was a glow of faith and love that flowed from her in spite of pain, and I knew she was loving and good.

I reminded her of this; then I asked, "Could you take this spirit of power and love and self control out of your life and explain how you have lived up to this moment? What a difference your life would have been without these. Your life has taken on a beauty and has been an inspiration because of them. You have drawn on God's power all your life. Now, rekindle the gift of God that is in you. Call on God for more power and love and self control. You cannot live for a moment in your own strength. God will continue to bless and beautify you for you have lived graciously in faith until now. In these very moments when you are filled with doubts and fear, put even greater faith in God; and he will bless you."

We had prayer together, and she prayed that God would renew his gift of faith in her. Some weeks later another cousin wrote and said, "Alice is more like her old self again—truly a joy to all of us."

Most of our problems are not due to bad things that happen to us on the outside, but because they cause a breakdown in the inside. We cannot handle our problems, or our pains, or our bad tempers by ourselves. They are on the inside. Paul's words are to the point. "Rekindle the gift of God that is in you." Take hold of this power. God did not make us to be weak or to let life get out of control. We can open the floodgates of his power and experience his steadfast love so that we can handle whatever may come to us.

We may need this in the middle of the night when pain or loneliness or discouragements overwhelm us. We may need it to help us be cheerful through days and weeks when we have reason to feel miserable. God is ready to supply that power and love. Draw on what God wants to do for you and receive his help today!

STEADFAST LOVE

Psalm 136, Ezekiel 18:30-32

You and I can never fully know the tragic suffering that was behind many of the beautiful Negro Spirituals. Slavery was an awful thing and out of the agony of hopelessness, there emerged a faith and a glory that speaks of the unconquerable spirit of those who were held captive. "Nobody knows the trouble I've seen, nobody knows my sorrow." True! But those further words are so unexpected, "Glory Hallelujah!" As the slave reached out for something to hold onto during those tragic years, he found it in his power to praise God, in spite of it all. Troubles, sorrows would come, but he had discovered the steadfast love of God and that did not let him give way. "Glory Hallelujah!"

You may be familiar with an early translation of the Hebrew word "hadesh"—lovingkindness. The lovingkindness of God spoke of his mercy and was a kindly concept. It reminds me somewhat of Josh Billings' definition of faith. He compared faith to a ship riding at anchor in a quite harbor. That is good enough when everything goes well, but what of times of trouble and sorrow—especially of slavery. Here we need a God, who is not a fair weather God, but who by his very nature is dependable, faithful, everpresent—steadfast.

From their beginning, the Israelites had experienced God's lovingkindness. They remembered that they had been slaves in Egypt and it had been because of his lovingkindness they were able to return to the promised land. But a time came when the very Temple of God had been destroyed and they had been carried into Babylon in chains. In their captivity they rediscovered God. In the midst of their troubles and sorrows they found they were able to sing because they began to realize that in all the changes that had come to them, God had not changed. Here was the moment when the "lovingkindness" of God began to be viewed as his "steadfast love."

117

Through the prophet, God said to them, "Repent and turn from all your transgressions, lest iniquity be your ruin. . . . Get yourselves a new heart and a new spirit! Why will you die, O house of Israel? For I have no pleasure in the death of any one, says the Lord God; so turn, and live." (Ezekiel 18:31f.) "Glory Hallelujah!"

A psalmist who lived at the time of Ezekiel, or shortly after him, reinterpreted their entire history. (Read Psalm 136) The steadfast love of God, or his mercy, showed through all that had happened in the past. It had prompted God to create the heavens and spread out the earth. It was manifest in the sun, the moon and the stars, "for his steadfast love endures for ever." That same love had rescued them from Egypt after dividing the Red Sea, and led them through the wilderness into the promised land, "for his steadfast love endures for ever." God was present, even as the psalmist wrote, to rescue them from all their foes. So they could sing, "O give thanks to the God of heaven, for his steadfast love endures for ever." And we would add, "Glory Hallelujah!"

In all the manifold changes of life, we humans change but God's love is unchanging. When Jesus taught his disciples to pray, "Thy Kingdom come, Thy will be done on earth as it is in heaven", he was calling them to rise above their shifting loyalties and appropriate the steadfastness of God. God's will is an overpowering, unchanging love. We may in our ignorance ask that the righteous be favored and those who are evil be destroyed. But there is a redemptive purpose in God's steadfast love, so the rain falls on both the just and the unjust. Because of God's steadfast love Jesus came not to destroy but to fulfill, to bring life and bring it more abundantly.

In the Garden of Gethsemane, Jesus prayed that the cup might pass from him, even as you or I might want to find a way out of a tragedy or be reassured in a moment of doubt. But there followed the cross. Here is the highest expression of the truth of the negro spiritual, for here, indeed was trouble and sorrow, but "Glory Hallelujah!" after pain and death came the resurrection. Good came out of tragedy because of God's steadfast love, and it continues to come to all who avail themselves of the living presence of Christ— God's most perfect expression of his steadfast love.

Rufus Jones, the great Quaker mystic of a generation ago, knew this steadfast love. Once when he went to Scotland to give a series of lectures, when he arrived at Liverpool he was handed a telegram that read, "Lowell (his son) is desperately ill." A second telegram arrived a few hours later. "Lowell is gone." Jones had strength and fortitude for even this dark moment. In the weeks that followed a ray of light broke through. The boys in Lowell's school set up a memorial fund and established the Lowell Jones reading room in the Boy's School in Ramalla, Palestine. Possibly the greatest discovery we can make is that suffering and insecurity can often be redemptive.

I have found this true in numerous times and places. My wife's sister looked out one day and saw her two-year-old run excitedly to watch a truck backing into the yard. The next moment David was crushed beneath the wheels of the truck. Word went out that rather than the usual flowers, a memorial fund would be sent to India. Some months later it was my privilege to open the David Perry Children's Room in the Bidar Hospital. It continues to be a blessing to sick children in that distant land.

A neighbor of the Perrys heard what had been done. She gave instructions that at her passing much the same was to happen. When she died a year later, those gifts were sent; and it was possible to establish a children's playground in the heart of an Indian city. Steadfastly the love shown at a time of trouble and sorrow has helped countless children say, "Glory Hallelujah!"

We need to look for this. Out of life' worst tragedy that befalls us there can be a redemptive and meaningful end when we draw on God's steadfast love.

What burdens are lifted from us when we lay hold of this steadfast love. It may well be that "nobody knows the trouble I've seen, nobody knows my sorrow," but among all those who have endured so much and have known God's steadfast love, their words are "Glory Hallelujah!"

IF WITH ALL YOUR HEART

Micah 6:6-8

A teacher tried and tried to get one of her pupils to study and learn until she was about to give up. One day, when the children were in a swimming pool, she took hold of the little boy and deliberately held him under water a few moments. He thrashed about and came up coughing and sputtering. When he could get his breath, she asked, "When you were under water, what did you want more than anything else?" He replied, "Air, I had to have air." Then the teacher said, "When you want to learn as badly as you wanted air, you will learn."

We may not have a problem learning, but there are times when we need help. Then we cry out in desperation, "O God." It may be a pain almost more than we can bear, or loneliness, or we may be so confused or frustrated we hardly know which way to turn, and it seems as if there is no one to help. In our inadequacy we cry out, "O God." The writer of one of our great Oratorios has taken words he found in the book of Jeremiah and put them this way. "If with all your heart you truly seek me, you shall ever surely find me, thus saith our God." Like the boy wanting air, if we want to find God with all our heart, eagerly, we shall ever surely find him.

You may laugh at an experience that came to me when I was a little boy. It was no laughing matter to me then, and it remains a vivid memory to this day. I wanted God, oh, how I wanted him, and I found him.

It happened when I was nine. We had always lived in town, but on that day my father had taken me to the country and left me with a family while he went on to call on church members. Then the family where I had been left were called away, and I was there alone on that big, wild farm—wild to a town boy. It probably hadn't been long, but to me it seemed like hours, and my father had not come for me. I decided to walk back to town, so I started out. After about a mile I turned a corner and there almost in front of me were a dozen or more cattle that had broken through the fence and were grazing along the road. I was terrified. I had to go down that road and those cows looked so terrible and big. There was only one help I could think of so I knelt, using the roadside bank as sort of an altar, and I prayed. I don't know what I said, but when I got up I felt I was not alone. I quickly surveyed the situation. All the cows were in the road, so I climbed the fence and walked in the pasture. Some cows lifted their heads and one or two started towards me out of curiosity, but very soon I had passed them and then I really walked fast. A few minutes later a car stopped and picked me up and delivered me safely back in town and all was well. As a terrified little boy, I knew that God was very near, and such awareness has come many times since then. "If with all your heart you truly seek me, you shall ever surely find me, thus saith our God."

An experience that came to Art Smith of Georgia was very similar. The details were vastly different, but God came into the picture much the same way. Art was engaged to a lovely girl when he was drafted into the Air Force; and after his training he became a rear gunner on a bomber. He tells how, time after time, when a Japanese plane came into his range he sent the plane down in flames, and how, every time that happened, it almost tore his heart out, for he thought how terrible to kill some other mother's son. He never fired the gun without saying, "Forgive me, God," but he knew that if he did not shoot down the enemy, he and the whole crew would be destroyed. At last he said to God, "If you let me come through this, I will give five years of my life to help save some of the boys and girls of the Pacific, instead of killing them."

That was how I got to meet him. After the war, he went home, studied to become an architect, married, had a small family, and at last came to India. He gave five years using his architectural skill. He built churches, schools, and hospitals. For Art Smith this was his worship of God. In desperation he had pledged those years to God. Today his buildings are monuments to worship, to learning, to healing all over India, testifying his response to God. "If with all your heart you truly seek me, you shall ever surely find me, thus saith our God."

We go back to the prophets. Ahaz was king in Jerusalem, and his enemies were threatening to take his kingdom from him. On his way to examine his fortifications he met the prophet Isaiah, who told him that even though he had strong walls, if his heart was faint, if he did not put his trust in God, then he would fail. Ahaz did not listen.

A neighboring king, who was also threatened with war, took one of his sons and killed him as a sacrifice to his god, attempting to show his willingness to make any sacrifice to assure victory. In like manner, Ahaz ordered his servants to bring one of his sons, and he built a great fire and placed his son in it as a sacrifice. It was not long after this the prophet Micah confronted the king and told him how wrong he had been.

121

With what shall I come before the Lord,
And bow myself before God on high?
Shall I come before him with burnt offerings,
With calves a year old?
Will the Lord be pleased with thousands of rams,
And with ten thousands of rivers of oil?
Shall I give my first-born for my transgression,
The fruit of my body for the sin of my soul?

Then came those tremendous words from the prophet,

He hath shown you, O man, what is good;
And what does the Lord require of you
But to do justice, and to love kindness,
And to walk humbly with your God.   (Micah 6:6-8)

Do justice. Amos, an earlier prophet had said, "Hate the evil, love the good. ... Let justice roll down like waters and righteousness like a mighty stream."

Love kindness. Jesus was later to say, "He who says he loves God but hates his neighbor is a liar, for God is love." When we reach out to serve others who have problems similar to our own, we experience that love. Love kindness.

Walk humbly with your God. I like the story of the widow's mite. There are ways that even the humblest and those who are themselves in need can worship God. When this widow gave all that stood between her and starvation to God in worship, she reached out in eager trust to God. "If with all your heart you truly seek me, you will ever surely find me, thus saith our God."

We need to remember when at times God seems far away and we grow fearful when we attempt to face our problems alone, that if we want God as desperately as the schoolboy wanted air we will ever surely find him. He has made us that promise.

THE TRANSFORMING POWER OF GOD

Psalm 19, Matthew 6:26-29

Life is a mystery. God has made us in such a way that we can take the good and bad, the delight of achievement, and the pain of failure and, with God's help, we can transform them into a beautiful life. How often, though broken by pain, we have learned to smile. In fact there is evidence that in a significant number of cases suffering adds to the quality of life and in not a few it stirs up compassion and stimulates the desire to be helpful.

God has a way of helping us take a hostile world and make it serve us. We see this lived out in the world about us. Among the beautiful flowers of the world are lilies. It is a mystery how water lilies and, in fact, most growing things, are able to sink their roots down into the slime and mud and black soil and draw up the food, the colors, the chemicals that sustain life and create beauty. We are moved to say, "Thank you God for these mysteries that you have put here for our delight and for our good."

What happens in the plant world can happen to us, to give life and nurture to our personalities and our spirits. One of my former professors, Dr. William Stidger, told how this happened to Dobry.

Dobry became a Bulgarian artist who painted wheat fields and flowers and growing things with such color and natural beauty that they almost looked alive. The remarkable thing is that God had taken this youth and gave him the power to see and to create beauty. Dobry was born into a peasant family where there was hardly a chance in the world for him to become an artist. But Dobry was fortunate to have a grandfather who was eager to share his simple but profound wisdom with him.

One day when Dobry and his shepherd-boy companion, Asan, were out looking after the sheep, Dobry's grandfather came with the noon-day lunch stuck down into the wide sash he wore for a belt. They sat together and grandfather broke the long loaves of bread and divided them. As they were eating, grandfather said, "When you eat this bread you are eating months of sunlight, weeks of rain, bits of iron and other chemicals and minerals from the rich earth. You take this food God gives you and your body transforms it into energy. You run and are filled with music and laughter." Then he pointed to a farmer who had a bag of seed under his arm as he planted a field. As the farmer scattered the grain, grandfather said, "The farmer carries a whole field of blowing grain in his bag, for every seed is alive. He is carrying not only a field of grain but our next winter's bread."

He let them think about this for a moment and then drew from his sash a beautiful autumn leaf, which he often carried, and said, "You see the autumn leaf is rich in color, and in many ways it is the most prized leaf of all. Like the autumn leaf, I am growing old, but old age should be the most beautiful, the most colorful time of life. We have to transform the good things of life, like the plants do the food in the soil, to make the colors come out right; in old age we have rich color and charm."

Dobry heard such stories from his grandfather until everything he looked at was not just a flower or a seed or a piece of fruit, and he said, "I must use these hands of mine to paint what I have seen. I must transform the paint and clay into beauty. I want to make the life-transforming mystery of growing things shine through what I paint."

This did not come to him all at once, and when he tried to form things into the shapes he wanted, it was a real struggle. Not for some time did his mother discover that Dobry was trying to paint and shape the things his grandfather talked about, and she said, "Dobry, you are just a peasant boy. You were born to tend the sheep and plow the fields and plant the grain," and she warned him against dreaming that he could ever become a painter.

Then one Christmas night as they came from the Christmas service at the village church, Dobry fell behind the others; and all night long he worked to create a nativity scene. He used the ice and snow of the farm yard. He made Joseph look like a peasant—just as his grandfather looked. The oxen were like theirs on the farm. He included a playful goat very much like the pet they all enjoyed. It took him most of the night.

When his mother and others went to care for the animals in the morning, they saw how Dobry had taken snowflakes and ice and transformed them into a nativity scene that was so real and beautiful they were drawn to it. Quietly they knelt in reverence and prayed. After that they gave Dobry all the help they could; in time he became a great painter, turning color and art into beautiful life-like paintings of the wonders of God's world.

As we eat our bread we remember how God has transformed clods of earth, blended with his sunshine and rain, into food for you and me. Such transformation is almost miraculous. But there is even a greater miracle, for he can take our mistakes and our weaknesses, mixed with our humble talents, our feeble words, and the warmth of our hearts, and with his blessing we become joyous, gracious, kindly, smiling men and women. You and I may never be famous painters, but we can ask God to take what we are and what we have and let his radiant joy and kindly love show through everything we say and do. Then the miracle of God's transforming power will happen in our lives, as it did in Dobry's.

INDIFFERENCE

Exodus 3:7-22, Ezekiel 3:14; 34, John 10:10

In the familiar story of the Good Samaritan, both the Priest and the Levite are put in a bad light, because they were indifferent to the needs of a man who was a victim of foul play. When they saw the man lying on the road they turned away from his need and "passed by on the other side." They may have said, "I'm too busy," or "I don't care," or they may have breathed a prayer that someone else might come to his aid. But they did not act, as we expect humans to respond to tragic need.

Some time ago a New York paper reported that a woman had been attacked on a busy street. She was knocked down and beaten to death, and her assailants escaped. There were people everywhere— leaning out of windows, standing in doorways, passing by, but not one responded to her call for help. That is not an isolated case for with crime on the increase, such stories are told all too frequently.

Some of the changes that are taking place in our society tend to promote this kind of indifference. As a boy in South Dakota, I was never far from hospitality on the frontier of life. If we had to stop at a farmhouse, we were the center of almost a frenzied response, as members of the household tried to comfort or assist us in our need. This helped shape my life.

But our world is changing. Technology may make life easier, but it also makes it more impersonal. My older brother, when just a boy,

125

saw it coming. Mother tried to get him to practice the piano. His response was almost a prophecy. "When I grow up, we will have electric pianos and everything will be done by electricity." Indeed, canned entertainment over television replaces personal involvement. The auto and the plane erase distances, so our next door neighbors remain strangers. Specialists not only service our electronic homes but teach our children, treat our illnesses, and computerize our responses to change. This mechanical world threatens those spiritual qualities that make us civilized. Life is structured in zip codes and neat mathematical formulas; the spiritual quality is extracted from life; and we become cogs in a machine. We are less emotionally and socially mature. The finest qualities of our lives are in jeopardy.

We who are growing older, who pride ourselves in having grown up in a warmer, friendlier, more concerned environment are threatened even more than many others by this mushrooming indifference. We are more vulnerable to attacks. We are physically less able to go to the help of others; when we do, we are aware our efforts may backfire, and we could lose our security. We steel ourselves by saying, "I don't care," which often is a vocal effort to hide how much we really do care but are afraid to act.

Our spiritual heritage warns us against indifference for we have ingrained in us a prompting to respond to human need. None other than Moses, when he found shelter among the Midianites on Mt. Sinai, was at first indifferent when God called him. You remember, Moses had been raised in the court of Pharaoh, but one day he saw an Egyptian master strike down a Hebrew slave. Moses killed the Egyptian and had to flee. God found him keeping the flocks of his new father-in-law, Jethro. In his burning bush experience, Moses heard God say, "Go down Moses, tell Pharaoh to let my people go." Moses' first response was, "Who am I that I should go to Pharaoh and bring the sons of Israel out of Egypt?"

What if Moses hadn't cared? What if he had left the Israelites as slaves in Egypt? Take from human history the Ten Commandments. Remove for all time the spiritual discoveries of the Hebrew prophets and psalmists, to say nothing of the fact that Jesus was a Hebrew and fed his spiritual life on so much that those of his nation had learned about God. History has been changed because Moses was not indifferent. His caring made possible a whole chain of events that have changed history.

The caring, compassionate opening of the mind, heart, soul, and the social response to human need are what life is all about. Without such compassionate responses life is flawed and can never rise above a bare human existence.

This caring, compassionate response doesn't come unless it is cultivated. It has a distinct spiritual texture that emerges through continous personal involvement.

Ezekiel was a priest-prophet who shared the fate of the Hebrews when Jerusalem fell to the Babylonians. He was among the captives taken to that foreign land. He says it was when he sat where those prisioners sat, "overwhelmed among them," that he discovered not only their agony and suffering but his eyes were also opened to both God and man. Further spiritual discoveries followed that were to prepare the Hebrews to return from the Exile and were responsible for many of their profoundly spiritual contributions to all mankind.

Ezekiel spoke of God as a great shepherd of his sheep (Israel). "I myself will be the shepherd of my sheep, and I will make them lie down, says the Lord God. I will seek the lost, and I will bring back the strayed, and I will bind up the crippled, and I will strengthen the weak, and the fat and the strong. I will watch over; I will feed them in justice." (Ezekiel 34:15f.) Jesus was to take this deeply moving discovery about the nature of God and show that the Good Shepherd is not indifferent but is a God who cares very much. (John 10:12-16)

Walter Dudley Cavert tells of a young printer in Gloucester, England, Robert Raikes, who was filled with such a spirit of caring. He saw the terrible conditions of prisoners in British jails and, for twenty years, tried not only to help them but also to bring about prison reform. His best efforts met with failure largely because people were so indifferent. Then he approached the problem in a different way. He planned to keep youngsters from becoming criminals, so the jails would not be filled and the prisoners neglected. As he thought of what he could do he noted that crime was intimately related to their repressive industrial system. Large numbers of children were forced to work long hours during the week in mines and factories. They had no chance to learn; so he opened a school on Sunday. He hired women not only to teach children to read, but also to instruct them in the Bible. He did more. Some children needed shoes and clothing; others had to have lunches. To keep others from crime, he actually paid them to attend his schools.

That was the beginning of the Sunday School movement that is just now 200 years old. Before Robert Raikes died, more than 250,000 children were enrolled in Sunday Schools in England, and the movement had spread around the world.

This quality that was so evident in Jesus—a power to touch life and transform it—does not decrease with age. Our years of experience surely qualify us to make special and invaluable contributions to society. We are not indifferent; we must never lose that tenderhearted warmth of old age that gives our lives special dignity and worth, which are so much a part of our self respect. We are people who care.

This may take a very personal application. Indifference might permit us to be untidy and careless about our person. But there is the challenge to beautify our surroundings by being at our best. There is more. An indifferent action during the course of the day—a careless gesture, a thoughtless noise or action, may irritate and disturb others. Because we are caring people, we endeavor to brighten relationships, make others more comfortable, and we encourage them to do likewise. And if we are more physically dependent on others, there are ways we can make their work lighter and pleasant. Cheerful words of appreciation flow naturally from caring persons and reveal an inner warmth that can transform even the darkest day and glorify the most difficult task.

The world needs this kind of radiant living, this quality that is so much a part of our spiritual heritage. Our God is a God who cares, and we draw our spiritual warmth from him because he cares.

In this mechanistic, impersonal world, the future still belongs to those who nurture their souls and undergird their lives on spiritual qualities that overcome indifference. This is God's world; and far from being forgotten numbers in an unfeeling world, we are part of a company who care, who seek to release God's spirit of compassion in all that we think, say and do.

THE DIVINE "YES"

Mark 1:16-20, II Corinthians 1:15-22

You have heard the story of Ali Baba and the forty thieves. They were shut up in a cave that would only open when they spoke the right words. Ali tried many words, "Open wheat, open barley, open hot, open cold, open air, open fire," and finally Ali Baba hit on the right words, "Open sesame." The doors swung open.

The Apostle Paul said there is a magic word that opens a person's life and that word is "yes." In II Corinthians he speaks of Christ when he says, "All the Promises of God find their yes in him." In Phillips' translation it reads, "He is the divine 'Yes.'"

The Gospels are full of what happens when people say yes to God. Mark records what happened when Simon and Andrew, James and John said "yes" and left their nets to follow Jesus. Matthew was called from the tax collector's office. What they found in Jesus completely uprooted them and turned them into world citizens and Children of God when they responded to this divine "yes."

Many others who heard Jesus were held captive by their traditions. As is true of many who have somewhat a negative attitude toward religion, they had the idea that more often than not religion told them what they could not do, rather than challenge them to dynamic living. They had been nurtured on a religion that said, "Thou shalt not." No wonder their religion had become a burden.

The negative plays too great a role in our spiritual lives.

One of my professors told of his three sons studying around a table. The youngest was forever asking questions, and time after time the older boys would say, "No, no, do not bother us." After this had gone on for some time, the oldest, attempting to be wise said, "Sonny, you might as well know. This is a no, no world." Into that kind of a world, Paul said Christ had come to pronounce a divine "yes." "The promises of God find their yes in him."

Jesus, you remember, said, "I came not to destroy but to fulfill." To the commandment, "Thou shalt not kill," he went on to show what change comes to a person whose heart is filled with love instead of anger and evil intent. To the commandment, "Thou shalt not commit adultery," he offered such a high regard for womanhood that lust had no place. His outlook was not negative. Much that passed for religion

129

in his day, and in ours, failed to challenge life at its best. It was even possible to fulfill all the Law and the Prophets and still not touch the fringe of one's real potential. He urged his hearers to let the wonders of God's world and the vibrant life of humanity open up their lives to life-stirring responses that left no room for filth of body or mind and all other negativism. Then the promises of God would begin to find their yes in them.

We have not fully caught his spirit. Far too often we have campaigned against sin in a negative, narrow way, when we might have struck at its roots through a positive approach. Paul said, "Overcome evil with good," and that is the response to the promises of God that find their yes in him.

William Barclay says there is no greater argument for Christianity than a Christian. I was fortunate to meet Dr. E. Stanley Jones, a world evangelist of a generation ago, soon after I arrived in India. Few men or women in all the Christian centuries have even approached the magnificent way this man said "yes" to God.

There was no uncertainty about his yes. When he was but seventeen he had a profound religious experience in a revival meeting in Baltimore, where he lived. Very soon after, he responded to a call to go as a missionary to India. After some necessary training he went; and only a few months later he was told that he had incurable tuberculosis. They sent him home to die.

Brother Stanley, as we called him, had said "yes" to God, and he did not intend to die. His cure was almost miraculous. He returned to India to begin a ministry that touched the throbbing life of that sub-continent as well as the outstanding leaders and students of many countries of the world. He gained their confidence and won a hearing, because everywhere he went he made known that God was trying to say "yes" to the spiritual longing of every one of them. He boldly made known that "the promises of God find their yes in Christ."

I watched him first in a Round Table Conference in Hyderabad, the capitol of the Nizam's Dominions. Outstanding political and religious leaders sat together around a table to share their spiritual experiences and their longings. Most of them had not thought of religion as a positive force that changed life and they found it hard to put their experiences into words. Then they asked Dr. Jones what his religion meant to him and he opened up the way Jesus had been touching life over the centuries. It was a creative, transforming spiritual power that lets one discover his real worth and releases inner responses so he can say yes to life. No wonder, wherever he went, great throngs came to hear him.

On an important occasion he was asked to meet a large body of students in the Town Hall in Jabalpur. It was during the early days of national awakening and with it an almost fanatical revival of interest in India's historic religions. Students were in the vanguard of opposition to Christianity which many regarded as an importation from the West. They came prepared to challenge Brother Stanley and for a time they threatened to turn the meeting into a hostile camp, but Dr. Jones remained calm. Patiently he listened to all they had to say and, at last, asked permission to speak. They listened. Then he told how he had discovered the "yes" of God in Jesus Christ, but he added, "I want the best there is for my life, and I think you do too. If you have something better than Jesus to offer me, I will listen. Tell me." And there was silence for Brother Stanley had shown how "the promises of God find their yes in Jesus." No one could give a more challenging affirmation for life.

We need to say "yes" to God. Life is not rich and full when it is crushed or violated or unfulfilled. Our positive, dynamic responses should replace the negativism of unimaginative religion. The promises of God find their yes in him and come alive when we let them find their yes in us.

Special Day Celebrations

As people grow older they should not be deprived of the delight and enthusiasm associated with the celebration of national and religious holidays. There are always some who are unable physically to join in community-wide programs and for them especially, Chaplains and others responsible for religious services should arrange to celebrate such festivals.

The Special Day Celebrations included here focus mainly on the Christian calendar but to these may be added Independence Day, Thanksgiving, and celebrations of other festivals in the Jewish and Christian calendar, as well as other national holidays.

Advent—New Beginnings

Luke 2:1-20

For many of us, Christmas is the favorite time of the year. The very thought of Christmas brings back memories of families, decorations, colored lights, gifts, and so much more. It is surely a joyous season.

In many churches, the celebration of the Christmas season begins on the fourth Sunday before Christmas, and the period beginning then and running up to Christmas is spoken of as Advent. It is a good designation, for advent signals the coming of one of great importance. Advent speaks of a new beginning, a profound change. For us it signals the birth of Christ, an advent so extraordinary that all the years and all the events ever since have been dated from the time of his coming. Here was a new beginning in history as well as in personal experience.

This new beginning has changed our attitude toward life. We might think of God looking down on a troubled world and searching for a way to enter directly into the lives of his people, a way that would help set things right. He could see that the world had gotten all tangled up in things that corrupted and dissipated and destroyed the good. How could God step into human history and point the way so that eventually mankind could overcome those traits that forever keep cropping up to corrupt life?

Evidently of all the ways he could have chosen there was one he thought best. He sent his Son into the world as a babe, as a symbol of a new beginning in human life, for all mankind. Here was a way to bring the Son of God right into the lives of his people; as he came to live among them, first as a growing boy, struggling with all the boy problems of his day; then as a youth in a carpenter shop, having to support a widowed mother; and at last as the leader of men, touching life tenderly and with compassion, but with bravery and courage and sacrifice.

In Jesus we see what humankind is capable of. We understand what the psalmist had in mind when he said, "God made man a little lower than God." The most joyous part of Christmas is exactly this— with the coming of Christ, mankind had a fresh start, a new beginning; now each of us can be Christlike. This is the important part of Advent and it gives meaning to all the rest; and there is more.

Advent takes on an intimate and very deep meaning when we stretch out the word until it becomes adventure. Advent is a continuing new beginning—an adventure. It may add to our joy and satisfaction when we dwell on what I have said about Advent and the coming of the babe into the world, but we go beyond this if we let Advent signal a new beginning that can take place in us.

When a farmer was delayed on his way to church and arrived just as the congregation was dismissed, the farmer asked the first man who came out the door, "Is it over?" The answer was prophetic. "No," the man replied, "it is not over. The sermon is over, and now it is up to us. Now we have to put it to work. We are just beginning." The coming of Christ marked a turning point in human history. The adventure of real living had just begun, and it is up to us.

Life, to be exciting and full of meaning is an adventure; and with adventure there is risk. It includes the element of sacrifice, and above all there can be no adventure without personal commitment. Jesus was God's adventure into human life that involved risk and commitment in a new way. Ever since then the followers of Jesus have carried this adventure into every corner of the world.

I once heard Dr. Wilfred Grenfell tell about the adventure of his life. For a time I lived in England and on flights to and from the States we flew over Iceland, Greenland, Laborador and the St. Lawrence River. I often looked down on that cold frozen land and shivered. I knew what cold was for I had spent the winters of my childhood on the frozen plains of South Dakota.

Grenfell tells how he heard of those who made their living fishing in the frozen waters of the north Atlantic. Many of them lived in isolated villages up and down the coast. There were no doctors, no medicine, no one to care for their physical and spiritual needs.

He was a prosperous doctor in London. Among his patients were some who had little wrong with them, but who wanted his attention and his treatments. One day he took a fresh look at life and said, "In London, there are many who can do what I do. Out there, there is no one. I will go where I am most needed." It was an adventure of faith. It cost him the warmth and comfort and relative ease of London for the ice-tossed crossings of polar seas to bring relief to a forgotten people. Though his hair was gray when I heard him, he was going back, for he was the life-line and hope of those who had long been neglected. His adventure was giving them a new beginning.

You may have heard of Alice Freeman Palmer who went in among the women and children who were shut up in the poorest homes of Charlestown Harbor. They looked out on bare cement streets, often covered with ice and snow in the winter. They never had enough to keep them warm. She knew that they could not get away from those bare walls, and they had little or nothing to work with. But she insisted that they must look on life as an adventure, for that would make their lives worth while. There were a number of things she suggested. One was that they must not let a day go by in which they failed to find something of beauty. One mother, shut in-doors with her children, had gone all day without a glimpse of anything beautiful, though she had tried. Then, just as the sun came through the window at close of day, it formed a halo in the hair of her little child. The hair spread out the rich full colors that an artist could never paint. Her simple adventure turned a dreary day into one she could never forget.

You may ask, "Where is the new beginning for me this Advent season?" You may be troubled because our society is so given over to violence. It seems that all about us crime is on the increase; the product of individual prejudice, selfishness, greed, and downright meanness. Many of us feel powerless to tackle such hideous social evils, so our adventure may have to be a personal effort to add what we can to the good in human society—to take our cue from what God did when he sent Jesus to inject good in an evil world.

Our adventure may be simple. Each day of Advent let us recall some beautiful word or quotation that speaks of a new beginning of peace and goodwill, or search in a book or magazine until we find a helpful thought. The Bible is full of such inspiration. Each day quietly sing some song that lifts up your spirit. If you cannot remember the words, let the tune refresh you and make you glad. Each day, reach out in love and touch another life with compassion— a physical touch, or possibly just a word, or at least the warmest smile you can wear.

Before I made these suggestions, did you think your days of adventure were over? If you get into the Spirit of Advent, your adventures will just now begin. The best moments, the best years of your lives may still lie ahead, and they can be traced back to the Christ Child who came into the world to let loose a new beginning for you and me.

Robert Collyer prayed that our lives might be enriched and made beautiful. Let us join in praying for God's blessing on us this day.

> Prayer. O Father, this day may bring some hard task to our life, or some hard trial to our love. We may grow weary, or sad, or hopeless in our lot. But, Father, our whole life until now has been one grand proof of your care. Bread has come to our bodies, thoughts to our minds, love to our hearts, and all from your tender love. May you be so powerfully present that we become more like you, and may we so trust you all through the day and in the days to come that our trust will grow stronger and work its miracle of good health in body, mind and spirit. When at last our life's work is done, may we trust you for all eternity and be with you in the joy of your presence. In the spirit of Christ our Lord, Amen.

Christmas—A Christmas Communion Meditation

Matthew 26:20-30; II Corinthians 1:20

Christmas is a joyous season. Let this period of meditation and worship be full of joy. May we so fill our lives with the spirit of Christmas that everyone we greet will know that it is truly Christmas. Let us radiate the presence of Christ in our lives. These are moments of adoration and praise.

Some may feel that a communion service belongs more to the Easter season than to Christmas. That was true of a chorister in a large city church. She was accustomed to the pageantry of the shepherds and the coming of the magi. When the minister announced that there was to be a Christmas Eve Communion service, she almost rebelled. But she was there and she brought joy into the service. She sang the hallelujahs and knelt for communion. There was a song in her heart as she came from the service that night, for Christmas had taken on a more wonderful meaning.

She discovered some important elements of the communion service that were also what made Christmas so special. Just as that meal Jesus had with his disciples in the Upper Room was so meaningful, in part, because Jesus wanted to be near those dearest to him, so Christmas is a time when we draw our families together in love. More than our immediate families are involved. Through cards and letters we express our love to those who have touched our lives profoundly and have enriched us. The more we let loose this expression of love in the intimacy and depth of fellowship such as was present in the Upper Room, the more we observe Christmas.

Second, to share in this communion service in remembrance of Jesus is a fitting way to usher in Christmas. We do not know exactly when the early Christians first celebrated Christ's birth. The first great impulse that thrust the disciples out into the world in the first century centered around the crucifixion, the resurrection and the coming of the Holy Spirit at Pentecost. These experiences let loose an awareness of God's presence in the early Christian community that sent them forth, as Luke tells us, to turn the world upside down. (Acts 17:6)

It was probably Mary, the mother of Jesus, who contributed much to the early celebration of Christmas. She had been with the small company of believers in Jerusalem from the time of the first Easter and was a part of the early church. It must have been as they listened to her that they learned about the events of the birth of Jesus. She had kept all those things in her heart. And when they did begin to celebrate the birth of Jesus, they called it the Mass of Christ, or Christmas. The pageantry in the Mass is similar to our communion service and that certainly was the earliest celebration of Christmas. So our celebration of the Lord's Supper at Christmas is not only spiritually but historically a most meaningful way to experience the greater meaning of this season.

Third. John wrote his gospel at about the time the early Christians first celebrated Christmas. What impressed him most was that God had sent his Son as a gift to mankind. God's gift has inspired us to give. Giving is a central part of Christmas so we not only give to God, we give to each other. John put it this way, "For God so loved the world that he gave his only Son, that whoever believes in him should not perish but have eternal life." (John 3:16) Because of his love he gave a costly and precious gift; it is a deep conviction among us that we love him because he first loved us. (I John 4:19) Because we have received so great a gift we are moved to show love, to give gifts at Christmas.

I shall never forget the costly gifts a woman offered that so well illustrate what I have been saying. It was only a few days after Christmas when a great throng of world leaders met in the church I was serving in India. One of the speakers was Bishop Ward of China. The Japanese had overrun the eastern part of China, and thousands had left their homes and fled to the west to find a new life. The Bishop told of their hardships and suffering and asked that an offering be taken for the people of China. I was standing at one of the exits with a good sized basket to receive their gifts. I discovered a country woman standing before me. Country people often do not put their meagre savings in a bank but invest whatever they save in gold ornaments. They wear these ornaments on special occasions, and for this Christian woman this gathering was surely one of the most important of her life.

I was hardly prepared for what happened. This village woman stopped before me and began removing her gold ornaments and putting them in my basket. First there were her necklaces, then half a dozen or more gold bracelets. Then she took the rings from her ears and fingers and toes. Every piece of gold she possessed was placed in the basket. There were tears of joy on her face as she walked away. Her gift, in the name of Christ, for people in China she would never

138

see, took on the aroma of the perfect Christmas gift—a gift that cost and came from her heart.

We would, however, still miss the main part of Christmas if there was not more in our celebration than this, and we find it in the communion service. There are three parts to our celebration. We confess our sins and receive pardon. We partake of the bread for our comfort. But these gifts without the giver are bare. As we partake of the memorial we pray that we may "be filled with the fullness of his life, may grow into his likeness and may evermore dwell in him and he in us." The poet put it this way, "Tho' Christ a thousand times in Bethlehem be born, if he's not born in you, you are still forlorn."

The glorious thing about Christmas is the gift of Jesus. What a difference he brought to the world of his day. He let loose a positive, creative goodness—a vibrant power that transforms human life and will transform us, too. We can accept God's gift now and let joy loose in our hearts. He will release positive goodness in us that will fill our lives with joy—a Christmas gift that will add luster to us throughout the year.

In the communion service there are Christmas gifts for us, and as we share in the table of the Lord, we receive into our hearts the greatest gift of all, for "God so loved the world that he sent his only begotten Son. ..."

The New Year—The Most Dangerous Journey In The World

Matthew 2:12

On this New Year's Day we begin a new year with 365 days stretching out before us. No matter how wise we are, we cannot tell what lies ahead. Once when a lecturer came to town he announced that he would talk about "The most dangerous journey in the world." He had everyone guessing, and when he introduced his subject he added, "The most dangerous journey is not that of a prisoner trying to escape or a thrust into outer space in a space ship. It is the journey of day-to-day living." He went on to say that it is not dangerous necessarily because others are unfriendly, but it is dangerous because of inner conflicts and personal problems. Very few escape troubles and hardships that are enough to test our courage, threaten our security, and cause even the bravest to lose heart. Such experiences tend to pile up until they are almost too big to handle.

Troubles may begin with minor irritations. How often you wake up in the morning feeling that you can hardly crawl out of a warm, comfortable bed. What an effort to flex one's muscles that rebel or arouse the mind to breathe in courage and determination. Some days seem as difficult as climbing Mt. Everest. It isn't long before you are well into the most dangerous journey. About the only thing you are sure of is that there will be more struggles ahead, even though you are determined to be gracious, kind, compassionate, and true to the best that you know.

You find yourself facing forward much like the three Wise Men in the scripture. (Matthew 2:12) They had been to Bethlehem and seen Jesus and then "being warned in a dream...they departed to their own country by another way." True, you got through the past year, but what of the way ahead? You may have to chart out and follow a different route.

There will be moments of testing that will put heavy demands on you. Some of them may involve members of your own family. You may have to deal with those who, in spite of having things going for them, prove spiteful and unkind. You may have to endure conflicts that almost tear you apart, so you are tempted to act as they do. When the going is rough, if you are to get to the end of the year's journey in good shape, you, like the Wise Men, will have to return by a different way.

Or, your life may have lost its excitement and much of its meaning. I once talked with a man in New Hampshire who had lived in the same house all his life. He boasted he had spent only two nights during his entire life away from that house. How uneventful! It might seem possible to escape many of the dangers ahead by sheer boredom, but how dull. And there was a man over eighty years old who had kept a record of what he had done, only to decide toward the end of his life that there hadn't been much that was worth recording. During those 80 years, he had slept a full twenty-six. He had worked twenty-one. It had taken him 221 days to shave his face. Another 140 days were needed to pay his bills. Then there were twenty-six days he had scolded his children; they must have been glad for that. He had yelled at his dog two full days; but he couldn't count more than twenty-six hours when he had laughed—twenty-six hours out of eighty years! What a gloomy fellow he must have been, and what a dangerous journey it would have been to have him as a companion.

The most dangerous journey for some may involve a change in the way we think or act or relate to others. I recall a time when I looked in the mirror and didn't like the frown that I saw; and I said, "Wipe that frown off your face; put a smile in its place." That wasn't easy; it was like the message that got through to the Wise Men telling they had to return a different way.

Gloom and discouragement may make a journey dangerous. The story is told that the devil boasted he had things going his way in the world. He was so successful that he decided to get rid of many of his tricks; but there was one he would not dispose of—that was discouragement. If only he could get people discouraged, he could handle them. We can't let that happen. With God's help we can be cheerful. Jesus was a cheerful person. How often he said, "Be of good cheer." "Rejoice and be exceeding glad." "My joy I leave with you." With God's help your journey into the New Year will carry a cargo of joy. What a poet put on the walls of the cathedral church in Chester, England, would serve well as an advice each one of us should follow.

> Give me a sense of humor, Lord.
> Give me grace to see a joke,
> To get some pleasure out of life
> And pass it on to other folk. Amen.

The best preparation we can have to start the journey into the new year—to begin the most dangerous journey in the world—is to walk with a companion. In Psalm 118:7 we read, "The Lord is on my side to

141

help me." Between the world wars the Japanese invaded China and there was a great migration westward to set up their government in a safe place. Out of that dangerous journey there came a song that I have heard on at least four continents, and it speaks of walking with a companion.

> I will not be afraid;
> I will not be afraid,
> I will look upward,
> And travel onward,
> And not be afraid.

> His arms are underneath me;
> His arms are underneath me;
> His hand upholds me,
> His love enfolds me,
> So I'm not afraid.

Most certainly, as we start this journey we need not walk alone. his love enfolds us so we need not be afraid. You may find, like the Wise Men, you must return a different way or you may decide to get rid of some of the things that have brought unhappiness to you and others. You may be asking yourself how you can be rid of jealousy, meanness, selfishness, and a contrary spirit that makes you gloomy and permits you to say things you really do not mean. You may have to return a different way.

Begin the New Year right. Say, "With God's help I will set free his healing power and strength in my body and mind. I truly want his spirit to make this year different. I will put God in charge so that my words, my actions, my thoughts, my kindly touch will reflect that I am at peace with God. I want him as my companion on the most difficult journey in the world."

Lent—A Time of Discovery

Luke 19:1-10

Lent, in the Christian calendar, is the forty days, excluding Sundays, before Easter. Traditionally it has been thought of as a special period of self-denial. There are some who in an effort to prepare for such a period, engage in every form of sexual and moral license for a time just before Lent begins, then they attempt a strict observance of conventional religious prohibitions as sort of a penance for their riotous living.

Lent, really is not a physical thing but a spiritual discipline. We come closer to realize its true meaning if we think of Lent as a period of self-enrichment. It should not be a time of denying ourselves, except our corrupt natures, but rather a time to give ourselves over to every form of life enrichment that we often neglect during most of the year. Prayer and meditation may be special forms of enrichment that come naturally during this period.

Life, we know, flows in rhythms. There are times when we are active and agressive in most affairs. We find ways to express ourselves. At other times our moods change. We are reflective. We are quiet. We are less active.

During our active moods we keep putting many things off, hoping to do them later. Lent may be a time for us to catch up. It is especially appropriate to express gratitude to those who have refined and uplifted our lives. It affords time to jot down what has decisively helped put a moral and spiritual tone to what we do and say, so that others in the family may benefit from such expressions. Lent is not a spiritual vacuum, but a time for creative and gracious enrichment, as we reflect on the many ways God seeks to open up our lives.

Among all that was told of Jesus during those memorable weeks just before the first Easter, two matters deserve special attention. Luke tells us (Luke 9:51) that Jesus steadfastly set his face to go to Jerusalem. Here is one of the important secrets of life and applies in particular to our aim to make Lent a time of real enrichment. Almost everything of worth we do, is done, because we set our minds to it. That was true of Jesus, not only in small things, but also in the large, as at the pre-Easter period when he was aware of the growing opposition that centered in Jerusalem. He did not run away from his problems. He was prepared to meet them unafraid. There was nothing cowardly about him. And it is truly amazing what we can

143

accomplish when we rally the force of our minds and hearts. Lent may be that special time during the year when we let the force of our character, our willpower and our minds, combine to turn our lives around and bring strength and beauty to all our relationships and our person. We should not be satisfied with anything less.

The second that deserves our attention is similar to what happened to Zacchaeus of Jericho, when he went out of his way to discover what difference Jesus might make in his life.

Zacchaeus had spent most of his life as a tax collector, collaborating with the hated Romans, in his greedy pursuit of wealth. The Jews hated such tax collectors, and when they spoke of them, they associated them with sinners. That is what they said about Zacchaeus.

But Zacchaeus must have had some good in him. When he heard that Jesus was passing by Jericho he went out to see him, and much to the surprise of the crowd, Zacchaeus climbed a tree in order to get a better view. Not many of us would put aside our dignity and climb a tree to see a spiritual leader. Zaccheaus did.

When Jesus saw him he stopped and said, "I'm coming to your home today." What a stir that made! The crowd began to murmur and ask, "Would Jesus go into his house? Would he eat with a tax collector and a sinner?"

That was where Jesus went, and after he had gone in with Zacchaeus, something began to happen. We don't know all the details, but while they were talking Zacchaeus began to realize that while his life was full of rich things, it was empty of all that he had found so worth while in Jesus. What a powerful impression Jesus must have made on this power-hungry, rich man. He began asking himself what his gold and silver, his power and position actually amounted to, when compared to the compelling strength and mysterious spiritual power Jesus offered. He blurted out, "Here, take half of my goods to feed the poor;" then turning to the crowd who had pressed into his courtyard, he added, "If I have defrauded any of you, I will restore it fourfold." Here was a moment of life-enrichment—of transformation—of change that was possible when he opened up his life completely to God. Jesus watched it happen and rejoicing with Zacchaeus said, "Today is salvation come to this house. For the Son of Man came to seek and to save that which was lost."

Let this period of Lent be a time when you take a fresh look at

Jesus. Be prepared for something to happen for you will want to let go those things that keep you from being your best. Life-enrichment—this Lenten season expect something great to happen. Salvation isn't something that happens when our life on earth has passed. It begins now as we nurture it, and it mounts up day by day, adding fullness and meaning to our lives.

Palm Sunday—The Power of a Great Enthusiasm

Matthew 21:1-10

When we read the account of Jesus' entry into Jerusalem, we can almost feel the excitement of those who were caught up in that moving experience. They were acting under the power of a great enthusiasm such as one might experience at a championship game or an auto race. They did unpredictable things. Some took off their outer robes and laid them on the road. Others cut palm branches from nearby trees for the same purpose. It was their way of giving Jesus the "red carpet" treatment. Such a reception may seem strange to many, but it is a form of oriental courtesy still observed, as I have seen, when a prince lays his costly oriental rugs on a roadway where a respected guest is expected to walk. Here was an exhibit of joyous enthusiasm.

This warm and exciting procession was a spontaneous expression of their dedication and loyalty. They shared Jesus' eagerness to extend God's Kingdom and for this reason they had come to Jerusalem, so they could release their new fervor in the very center of their religious communal life—the Temple. They had heard Jesus' challenging words, "If any man will come after me, let him deny himself, and take up his cross, and follow me. For whosoever will save his life shall lose it, and whosoever will lose his life for my sake shall find it." (Matthew 16:24f.) It was an exciting response to this that fired them as they sang their hallelujahs and gave praise to God that day.

Our enthusiasm gives a vitality and excitement to our lives. A minister tells of going into a hospital only to be met by a stranger who ran up to him with the news, "It's going down! It's going down!" Day

145

after day this man had watched with dismay as his wife's temperature had been on the rise, but on that day it had started down. He was so excited he had to tell someone and the minister was the first he saw.

Excitement and enthusiasm are feelings all normal persons experience. How greatly we are stirred when we give ourselves to a deeply felt cause or stand firm for our convictions. Such enthusiasm draws us out of our shells. It releases pent up energies. We come alive under the power of a great enthusiasm.

On that first Palm Sunday, there were no doubt some in the crowd who waved their palm branches and shouted their hosannahs who, before the week was past, would be swayed by the enemies of Jesus, and then their shouts would be "Crucify! Crucify!" But on that joyous day, they were carried along with the others in their enthusiasm. Here was Simon the fisherman. Jesus had fired his enthusiasm, telling him he was to be a "fisher of men." Others had been drawn for other reasons but all were ready to lay down their lives for his sake. They could hardly realize they were at the beginning of a movement that was to stretch down succeeding generations; that would in time release the transforming love of God to the far corners of the world.

Such enthusiasm is still a mark of discipleship and there are places where it breaks out afresh from time to time. It is visible not only in the well established centers of the faith but on the frontiers of mission effort. I found it in India.

I arrived in India not long after the Telugu country in south central India experienced its first great wave of what has been called the Mass Movement. That movement brought thousands of Harijans (That is the name Mahatma Gandhi gave the untouchables) into Christianity. These unfortunates had been born into a hopeless degredation from which their only escape was death. But in Christianity they began to discover a new life and it filled them with a new enthusiasm. There is an exciting story behind that movement.

The missionary, Charles Parker, spent most of his missionary life in the villages of India. A few of his early converts had received an education and some training and were formed into a band of enthusiastic village preachers. But in spite of their best efforts, there had been little response. At last, Parker called these preachers together and asked them to make a final all-out effort to reach every person they could with two messages. First, they were to repeat John 3:16, pressing home the message that no person was despised in God's

146

sight and that God loved them so much he gave his own Son that they might have a full and joyous life now and eternally. Then they were to tell what Christ had done for them.

These village preachers went out fired with a new purpose. They talked with people on trains, along the roads, around village wells, and in their homes. The response was beyond all expectation. Village after village decided to become Christian and asked for instruction; the great Mass Movement of this century had begun.

Within one or two generations, the lives of the people in those villages has been transformed. Some of those early village preachers were leaders of the church when I reached India and I could still feel the power of their enthusiasm. From among their humble converts have come some of the spiritual giants of the Christian movement today. That is what happens when the power of a great enthusiasm lays hold of people.

You may say, all that may be well for others; but here in my condition the most I can do is to find strength to meet the demands of each day. You may be sure God does not expect you to carry the gospel out across the world; but God makes it possible for each of us to use our powers and act faithfully within the limits of our circumstances. In doing this we feel the excitement of doing his will.

There was a teacher in Ohio who taught for forty-five years in a two-room schoolhouse. Someone might say, "What a ghastly life, teaching stubborn children, correcting endless papers, year after year, through a lifetime." One day after her teaching days were over, she received a book in the mail, written by Dr. Gunsaulas of Chicago, one of her early pupils. On the flyleaf he had written, "To the one who opened the gates of life and literature to me." For forty-five years, she had carried her enthusiasm for learning into the classroom and had fired the enthusiasm of a great man. He had brought light and life to others.

How radiantly beautiful are those among you who dredge up, in spite of physical limitations, a growing enthusiasm because of your personal response to God. Every gracious act becomes a palm branch on the roadway for another who may desperately need to feel the enthusiasm of your strong faith.

When a man went into a store, he asked for a compass. The clerk inquired, "What kind of a compass do you want?—the kind that draws circles or the kind that gets you some place?" Many of our enthusiasms just make us go in circles. They don't get us any place. But Jesus' invitation is for those who want to get some place. He challenged them. He not only aroused their enthusiasm but he provided the power that gave meaning to their lives. And that is the power of a great enthusiasm.

The hymn writer must have had this in mind when he wrote,

Were the whole realm of nature mine,
That were an offering far too small.
Love, so amazing, so divine,
Demands my life, my soul, my all!

Good Friday—The Seven Last Words

Recorded in the gospels are the seven saying of Jesus as he hung on the cross. They are not in the form of a discourse, nor are they his last will and testament. Rather, they are the cry of one undergoing the most cruel death that could be inflected on anyone. He was nailed to a cross and the cross lifted high and let drop into the hole dug for it. Then while the soldiers guarded it and the carnival crowd watched his agony, Jesus suffered and died. A righteous and good man suffered; the Son of God suffered and died for the sins of the whole world. Among those near the cross were some who listened, and we note here the words they heard.

"Father, forgive them, for they know not what they do."
(Luke 23:34)

The disciples on one occasion asked Jesus to teach them to pray, and Jesus included in the prayer these words, "Father forgive us. . . as we forgive those who trespass against us." Then he added, "If you do not forgive men their trespasses, neither will your Father forgive your trespasses." Now his prayer was being tested. Those who nailed him to the tree had done the cruelest thing they could, and he was ready to forgive them. His words and his life were one and the same.

When he asked God to forgive them, whom did he have in mind?— those who drove the nails into his hands and feet? Did he include

148

Pilate, that vacillating Roman, who could have saved him? Was Herod, the crafty Jewish ruler to be forgiven? What of the religious leaders, Annas and Caiaphas? In asking for his death, had they attempted to protect their power and privileges? What of the scribes and pharisees—the religious "right" of his day, whose limited religious concepts stirred up the masses "in the name of God," in support of their prejudices and superficial worship. Did he include the disciples who had run away? Were there others? Jesus was suffering because of all of them, yet he could pray, "Father, forgive them."

We are inclined to draw attention to the evil we see in others in order to make our own record appear better. But Jesus, while hanging on the cruel cross, showed supreme goodwill and a generous spirit when he graciously said, "They know not what they do." This severely challenges us. Does it mean that even when we are filled with "righteous indignation" we must make room for pity? Need we be on guard lest our indignation when "fighting" vice and crime, drives out compassion for the evildoer? Not only during the years of the Inquisition have those who hunted out "heretics" been more lacking the spirit of Jesus than many of those they accused. What a lesson for all of us. Jesus, here on the cross, seemed aware that any lack of a forgiving spirit would violate God's plan to redeem mankind. His first word set things right. He forgave them. Thereafter he was prepared to handle whatever else was to come.

"Truly, I say to you, today you will be with me in paradise."
(Luke 23:43)

There were three crosses on that hillside. Three were to die that day. Their physical suffering was probably much the same. Three lives were snuffed out. But what a difference in their deaths.

Jesus died because he sought to give life and stood against evil, even when it wore religious garb. Near him were two thieves who, according to their own testimony, were being punished because they had done others wrong. They embodied evil. "The two thieves were crucified because they hated men," Talmage C. Johnson writes, "because they sought to take life, and because they dared resist good. ... Hatred incarnated in them attempted to destroy love incarnated in Jesus. ... Jesus was crucified because he loved men, because he sought to give life, because he dared resist evil. ... Thus, though the thieves shared the suffering with him, they also caused his suffering.

149

Evil kills both its friends and its foes. It is death; it can never give life. Good is life; it can never take life."

But one of the world's most moving dramas was played out on those crosses that day. The gospel reports it.

One of the criminals who were hanged railed at him, saying, "Are you not the Christ? Save yourself and us!" But the other rebuked him, saying, "Do you not fear God, since you are under the same sentence of condemnation? And we justly, for we are receiving the due reward of our deeds; but this man had done nothing wrong." And he said, "Jesus, remember me when you come in your kingly power." And he said to him, "Truly, I say to you, today you will be with me in Paradise."

Three crosses, yet three who were so different! Jesus, who offered forgiveness to his enemies; a thief who was entering eternity bitter and unrepentant, carrying the weight of his sin. The other thief, who had been made aware of God's mercy and grace when he saw it reflected in Jesus, now repentant. God's forgiveness could not erase the consequences of his sin, but his guilt was set aside. His soul was accepted at last.

"Woman, behold your son. ___ (John) behold your mother."
(John 19:26f.)

No doubt Jesus' mother had followed him from the time of the trial or before. Now as Jesus looked down on her, he rose above suffering to show compassion and care. This one who had given him life now needed someone to watch over her. John must have found it a great privilege to stand in for Jesus in that most sacred family responsibility.

In a way his mother was a symbol of all the helpless of the world, for had he not said on another occasion, as he stretched out his hands toward the disciples, "Here are my mother and my brothers! For whoever does the will of my Father in heaven is my brother, my sister, and mother." (Matthew 12:49f.)

This fellow-feeling is an amazing part of Christianity. As a missionary far removed from my family, I have never lacked the warmth and tenderness of such love, which is so uniquely Christian. It overreaches race, nation, and gender. It was born right there on the cross, and it belongs at the very center of all that the cross stands for in today's world.

"My God, my God, why hast thou forsaken me?"
(Matthew 27:46)

At first, when we hear these words, we might conclude that Jesus had lost his composure and that this was a cry of desperation. The circumstances would seem to warrant it. Had that been the case, his voice would have been added to all those through the centuries, who, when caught in some tumultuous difficulty, had asked, "Why should this happen to me?"

Some standing near might have concluded that this was what Jesus meant. So much had happened. His trusted disciple, Peter, had denied him. Judas, one of the twelve, had sold him for thirty pieces of silver. The others had fled, and many who had shouted "Hosannah" just a few days earlier were among those who were heard to cry, "Crucify, Crucify!" Where in all this was there evidence of God's mighty power over evil?

From a purely human point of view this might seem plausible but I am confident the truth lies elsewhere. These words are the opening declaration of a great Psalm. In the twenty-second Psalm they do not stand alone but are a prelude to an affirmation of God's faithfulness to the Hebrew nation. In his moment of crisis the whole prophetic Psalm came back to provide him with powerful imagery of God's faithfulness and continuing support. These verses, in particular must have spoken to the situation.

My God, my God, why hast thou forsaken me? Why are thou so far from helping me, from the words of my groaning? O my God, I cry by day, but thou dost not answer: and by night, but find no rest. ...
In thee our fathers trusted; they trusted and thou dids't deliver them. To thee, they cried, and were saved; in thee they trusted, and were not disappointed. ...
Since my mother bore me thou has been my God. Be not far from me for trouble is near and there is none to help. ...
Thou dost lay me in the dust of death. ... They divide my garments among them, and for my raiment they cast lots. But thou O Lord, be not far off. O thou my help, hasten. ... deliver.
He has not despised or abhorred the affliction of the afflicted, and he has not hid his face from him, but has heard when he cried to him.
Dominion belongs to the Lord, and he rules over the nations. ...
Posterity shall serve him; men shall tell of the Lord to the

151

coming generation, and proclaim his deliverance to a people yet unborn, that he has wrought it.

Experiences do occur that make us feel we are passing through the "dark night of the soul," but we must not allow ourselves to be creatures of these desperate moments. We must remember other times, better circumstances, when God has proved the very foundation of our lives. Jesus did. He recalled the implicit trust of his forefathers. They were confident that no matter what suffering some might endure, God would triumph in the end. This greatly comforted him as he hung on the cross.

"I Thirst."
(John 19:28)

The agony of the cross shows up here. Jesus was not play-acting. He was not a pawn on the chessboard of history. He was human and this was an urgent need, for he was thirsty.

Some have suggested that this was a spiritual thirst. It hardly was that. Had he not told the woman of Samaria, "Everyone who drinks of the water (of Jacob's well, where she had come to draw) will thirst again, but whoever drinks of the water that I will give him will never thirst. (John 4:13f.) Jesus possessed the water of eternal life, and he said, "If any man thirsts, let him come to me and let him who believes in me drink. ... Out of him shall flow rivers of living water." (John 7:37fb)

Jesus was thirsty. No doubt Jesus was appealing to the Roman soldier who stood near-by. It is sometimes thought degrading for us who are growing older to ask help from others. If and when a time comes that we cannot meet our physical needs, we, like Jesus, should call out for help.

In truth, we are all interdependent. No one could have eaten breakfast this morning without the help of a vast number, most of whom we will never see or know. There were those who kept the dairy from which the milk came. Others milked the cows, transported the milk, delivered it to us. The same was true of our cereal, fruit, and coffee. Moment by moment we depend on others, for we are interdependent. When we are in need, we must call out. Jesus did, when he said, "I thirst."

"It is finished."
(John 19:30)

The word used here does not say, "This is the end;" rather, "I have finished the work God gave me to do." Some would see here only a young man, approaching the prime of life, whose career had suddenly been cut short when he was arrested, tried, and then hung between two thieves. There is more in this declaration than that he had given up.

In the garden, Jesus had prayed, "Not my will but thine be done." As events unfolded, his Father had given him strength and composure. Now, through Jesus on the cross, God was stepping down into history to make known his salvation in a completely authentic way. That act was now accomplished. God had been incarnated into human history. "For God so loved the world, that he gave his only Son, that whoever believes in him should not perish but have eternal life." (John 3:16) This work was finished.

There was also, in this hour, the triumph of a spirit completely dedicated to God's kingdom and its advancement among men, as the ultimate working out of God's will. Jesus' physical suffering was as nothing compared to this. Both his spirit and God's spirit triumphed for they shared this agony together.

"Father, into thy hands I commend my spirit."
(Luke 23:46)

Nor are these the words of resignation or defeat. Rather there is here an affirmation of oneness with the Father. Even as he had affirmed God's will when at work among men, now he could enter God's presence unafraid. It is as if he were saying, "Now I begin to see what it is all about. I accept it, not as something imposed on me, but willingly, as one with the Father, as we work things out together for all mankind."

Again, these words came out of his heritage. They were words a Hebrew mother often used with her child. As the evening shadows fell, she would draw her child to her and repeat these words much as we are taught, "Now I lay me down to sleep, I pray the Lord my soul to keep." That prayer the mother used with her child, "Into thy hands I commend my spirit," was an early form of the same prayer. Now on the cross those words from his childhood sprang to his lips to give utterence to his complete oneness with God. What greater prayer could anyone utter at that moment when he passes from this life into the next.

These seven words on the cross engage our imagination and stir our dedication. Here is faith played out on a living canvas. As we reflect on them they help turn us from being spectators of a crucifixion to become participants in God's redemptive plan for mankind. It was for us Christ died, and we have been deeply moved as we have felt both the tragedy and the triumph of his sacrifice on the cross of Calvary.

Easter—The Easter Flame

Matthew 28:1-10

There are two places in Jerusalem that are said to be the tomb of Jesus. One is a rocky burial cave on a hillside in a quiet garden. Its tradition does not go back very far, but it has much to support it. The other is down in what is a busy part of Jerusalem, and is known as the Holy Sepulchre. It is a fort-like structure, almost black with age. In it are several grottos, each owned and maintained by different religious groups and each is said to be the original tomb. At an early date Christians built a covering over what they thought was the actual tomb and this has been enlarged into a great building covering the traditional site.

In this church there is the Roman Catholic tomb—richly decorated and maintained by a continuous procession of priests and monks. Near-by is the Eastern Orthodox tomb with its decorations and priests. There is also an Armenian tomb and others of shorter tradition belonging to different Protestant groups.

In one of the shrines—I do not remember which—on Easter morning just as the first light appears in the eastern sky, a flame bursts forth into brilliance. It appears as the final words of Stabat Matre are sung. No doubt the priests control it in some way, but local people still believe it is a miracle. There is always a crowd waiting for the flame. People rush forward, light their candles and small lamps and go out carrying the flame into the early morning light. Some quickly mount horses to take the sacred fire to congregations in near-

154

by villages. The fire symbolizes that Easter has come, that Christ arose from the dead that first Easter.

The gospel accounts do not mention an Easter fire, but they do tell of the brightness of the tomb and the radiance of the clothing. Certainly the symbolism of fire is very ancient. It expresses vitality, purity, and spirituality. The Spirit and the flame are almost one, and they are far closer to Easter than the Easter rabbit, the colored eggs, and the display of fine clothes in the Easter parade.

The flame symbolized the presence of the Spirit. When both Isaiah and Jeremiah received their calls to prophecy, they stood speechless before the throne of God. Isaiah saw the Seraphim take coals from off the altar and touch his lips. Isaiah went out on fire for the living God; and we often speak of being on fire, or having the Spirit of God burning within. We especially associate the flame with the coming of the Spirit to the company of believers at Pentecost. Pentecost and the open grave, together, gave birth to Christianity. Jesus stepped forth from the grave as "the light of the world."

We need that resurrection flame each Easter. There is rich symbolism here in the entire Easter event and particularly in the release of Jesus from the tomb. At Easter time, we think again of the deeper lessons we may learn from those events.

First, the tomb reminds us that Jesus was crucified by violence and crime and these are present in our social structure to destroy spiritual vitality today; evil forces still minimize godly efforts to relieve human misery, thwart social justice and righteousness, and run contrary to what we have learned from the prophets and Jesus. The Easter flame reminds us that this is God's world and that although the good loses out for a time, the day of resurrection will come, and the same power that brought Jesus from the grave, as St. Paul so often reminds us, will in the end see that justice, peace, and righteousness triumph.

Second, we would note that materialism now threatens to entomb our spirits. In many ways we have permitted our spiritual natures to degenerate as we have become victims of selfish and physical desires. We have almost deified comfort, convenience, and ease. We are more fearful of what may happen to our bodies and our physical world than what is happening to our spiritual understanding. We give little attention to the dynamic release of God's power in the world. We shy away from hardships for Christ's sake or from anything that calls for personal sacrifice or the upholding of righteous convictions. No generation escapes this entirely but in our generation far too many have entombed much that pertains to Jesus' way of life. Easter reminds us that this should not be so.

Third, we are helped when we remember that St. Paul often spoke of "the power of the resurrection" as a power that transformed the weak and terrified disciples and made them men and women of courage and inexhaustable energy. The same power that raised Jesus from the dead had done that, and it is available to work its spiritual transformation and victorious release in us. The conflicts of our inner lives, our feelings of frustration and loss, our inadequacy to meet the demands of today, our feeling of powerlessness to change those things in the social structure that ignore moral and spiritual standards, are all very devastating. At Easter we remind ourselves there is power available so we can deal with these matters. We need to lay hold of it. Though his contemporaries locked Jesus in the tomb, the rocks and the grave could not imprison his spirit. The resurrected power of Christ sets us free. If sin overwhelms us or we are in trouble, we can break the bond of sin through Christ's resurrected power and be restored to a joyous life again. If our lips speak evil or our minds harbor vain thoughts, or our hands work harm; the resurrected power of Christ will free us from inhumanity and greed and break open the grave of indifference, as we think again of brotherhood and the welfare of others. The Easter flame may have burned dim in our souls, but Christ is waiting in the dawn to give it new life once again.

Fourth, each year those who gather in Jerusalem at Easter time to light their candles in the Easter flame do so because the central message of Easter is one that verifies that our spirits are eternal. Death is not a terror to a Christian. Every divine encounter in life adds to the joy we will have eternally in the presence of God and the risen Christ. God has surrounded us from our birth with his steadfast love and through faith in Christ we accept the promises of God both for this life and for all eternity. We belong to that company in each generation who at Easter sing our Hallelujahs because we know that Christ is risen from the dead, and because he lives, we too shall live, Hallelujah!

Jesus could have come and been lost in history except for the flame of his resurrection power that burned in his disciples. That power comes afresh to each generation of believers. Every life he touches, he makes better. We find comfort, strength, healing, as we light the candles of our lives in his resurrection fire. He lives, and because he lives we too live now and eternally in the power of his resurrection.

Dealing with Stress

There is no magic that can take the place of the magnificent way God works through our minds and hearts to turn stress, tension, hardship, frustration, frailty into open doors of growth, wholeness, and the maturing of the soul. Such tensions that at first seem to be stumbling blocks can be turned into stepping stones for the refinement of one's whole person. For such a miracle to happen we must lay open our whole being to the steadfast love of God and deliberately pursue a course of growth that focuses on the healing of our minds and bodies with God's help.

The following are some of the more pressing tensions familiar to senior adults. You can change these stumbling blocks into stepping stones with God's help.

Growing Older

No matter how favorable my circumstances, as I grow older I can well expect to experience a number of losses. My eyesight, hearing, muscle flexibility, stored up energy, will not serve me as well. My family, friends, and social contacts will be restricted, due to deaths and changes in residences. The living arrangements I once considered essential will likely be beyond my resources. I will have more time but less energy for clubs, church, and social service projects. Undoubtedly there will be other important ways I will experience losses.

How can I keep such changes from taking away my dignity and the essential quality of life I value so highly? St. Paul, who must have been in late middle age or older when he wrote this, took a second look. He said, "Though our outer nature is wasting away, our inner nature is being renewed every day." (2 Cor. 4:16.).

I must not dwell on my losses and feel sorry for myself or my mind and spirit will not be able to discover new ways to enhance my wellbeing. I must learn how to utilize not only my remaining physical strength but also release my inner reservoir of mental and spiritual energy that will give me the most satisfying life possible.

There are important ground rules I must follow. The first is to move carefully and not sweep aways all the good and valuable relationships and activities that remain options.

A second is to adopt those pursuits that provide scope for maturing and growth during the coming years. To do this I may need to form new relationships and identify with persons and groups who are seeking to serve humanity through social reform, spiritual renewal, or outgoing service to others. I must become involved in ways that will take me out of myself.

Third, I will recognize the importance of a healthy body and good nutrition. I must exercise wisely to remain physically strong.

Fourth, I will survey my skills and my special aptitudes and begin to give expression to the special talents and skills I have, whether they be artistic, compassionate caregiving, or along other lines.

Fifth, it is said that often during earlier years the inner life of the spirit was neglected for what seemed to be more pressing demands. Now that I have the opportunity I will find ways to deepen my awareness of God and develop a clearer understanding of the meaning of life. My prayer life will be enriched and I will search the Scriptures and learn as best I can why God has given me these added years and how to use them in ways pleasing to him.

Life is such that some losses are inevitable. Those losses that come to me as I grow older are not entirely different than those that have happened earlier. Somehow I feel more vulnerable. This makes me realize that it is up to me. No other person can turn my losses into something good. It is my responsibility, yet not mine alone, for I am confident that it is God's gracious will that as long as I have breath, I will continue to be led by his Spirit and share the abundant life of which Jesus spoke.

Prayer.

My Heavenly Father, I give thanks to you for my length of days and for the degree of health and the many ways others have made it possible for me to have a privileged life. I thank you for parents, for family, for friends, for caregivers and others who have contributed to my welfare. I am supported and made glad as I accept your steadfast love that assures me that I am your child and precious in your sight. I thank you for your Son, Jesus Christ, who lived and died to show us the depth of your love and best of all how we can turn loss and defeat into fullness of life. Hear me now as I pray for your guidance and strength as I chart my course for the added years you give me. Help me to grow in body, mind, spirit, and in my service to those in need.

I give thanks that I am not alone as I chart ways to use these coming years in meaningful ways. I thank you for those who strive to give enriched meaning to all of life and who give of their time and energy to open up avenues for growth and involvement. I thank you for churches and other agencies that have directed me in my quest for divine guidance; for family and friends who lovingly support and comfort me, and for the faith that engages my whole being. Receive my thanks and give me your blessing. In the name and for the sake of Jesus Christ, my Lord. Amen.

Loneliness

When I am lonely I feel depressed. Although I have known loneliness during earlier years now it comes more often and is more of a problem. As I grow older I have experienced many losses. I cannot see or hear as well and I suffer more physically. I no longer have a job. I left my familiar neighborhood. Many of my family and friends have died or are far away. Like so many others I am lonely and often given over to despair.

Being alone is not all that bad. I don't have to answer to others when I am alone, and there is time to think and catch up with myself. When Jesus was in the Garden of Gethsemane, he was alone and he offered one of the greatest prayers ever expressed, "Not my will but thine be done." I think he was lonely, too, for he stopped praying and when he found his disciples he asked them to watch and pray with him, but they went back to sleep. His being alone may have been necessary, for there are some things we have to work out by ourselves. In his loneliness, Jesus trusted God to release inner resources to fortify him and calm his spirit so he could handle the tragic adversities that awaited him. I will never be in nearly as tight a spot as Jesus was. Later he assured his disciples that they would never know any loneliness or loss that would deprive them of the strength, insight, and love of their Heavenly Father.

All around me are those who need my help. If I offer a helping hand it will link me with at least one other person and this can take some of my loneliness away. If I can get started, one thing will lead to another, until I will be involved with others and doing things that add richly to their lives. Doing such ordinary things will bring extraordinary results and lift me out of loneliness.

There are others who are lonely. The bed-ridden and infirm often feel alone in the world. They feel deserted or neglected by family and friends and there is often no one to whom they can turn in their loneliness. While some of them who are more able reach out to others by phone or letter and so are not so lonely, there are many who must spend hours and days without the comfort of friends or the strength to do for themselves.

I have been inspired by the way some of them overcome loneliness. One such soul remembers poems or songs he once learned and his life is brightened as he repeats the great words or music from the past. Another retraces his life story, year by year, using part of each succeeding day to rehearse events and experiences in great detail. Another travels the oceans and the airways as he revisits lands and places distant and near, and encounters afresh those who brought joy to his life at an earlier time. Still another replays games of sport that delighted him, recalling the great moments and sometimes the embarrassing moments of sports that were a joyous part of his life. Still another traces his spiritual life story — his encounter with God through the Scriptures and in life, and the many ways God has drawn the best out of him and added to his place in the world. I have learned that even those who are dependent on others can overcome loneliness.

Jesus has promised to meet me in my need, "Lo, I am with you always to the end of the age." He is the shepherd looking after his sheep. I can sense his presence. Even now I am supported by his love. Thank God, I do not have to be alone.

Now as I pray this ancient prayer I am reminded that loneliness is not unique to my generation.

Lord Jesus, we beseech you, by the loneliness of your suffering on the cross, be nigh to all those who are desolate, in pain, or in sorrow today, and let the beauty of your Presence transform their loneliness into comfort, consolation, and holy fellowship with you. Lord Jesus, out of your pity, hear us. Amen.

O Lord, I have tried to find the cause of my loneliness. If it is within me, if there is stubbornness of spirit or unreadiness to venture forth in determined effort to surmount this feeling, show me how this may be done. If I am unable to act for myself grant that I may be found by others who will relieve me of this complaint. Give understanding to those who seek to serve the helpless that they will not only renew their hope but enable even those most impaired to feel their compassionate love and be relieved of their loneliness. Amen.

Sleeplessness

Sleepless nights do come. The body is fatigued. The mind is overburdened. At such a time my mind races to recall one event after another. I long for sleep but somehow I cannot turn off my mind. I remember a duty I must care for tomorrow. (I know it is good to have a note pad handy and write it down.) Then I get into the most comfortable position I can. I relax my muscles. I try to let go and feel relaxed.

To quiet my mind I pick up this brief note about God's steadfast love. I remind myself that God cares for me and that his care reaches out to all those I hold dear. I may be powerless to reach them in thought or word or to solve the pressing problems I face, so I ask God to touch my life and theirs and do what is best. I begin to feel composed and more at ease. The words of the Psalmist come to mind:

When I think of thee upon my bed, and meditate on thee in the watches of the night — in the shadow of thy wings I will sing for joy. Because thy steadfast love is better than life, my lips will praise thee. O God, thou art my God, earnestly will I seek thee. (Psalm 63)

Then I remind myself of the words of another Psalmist. "The heavens declare the glory of God and the firmament" — the earth — is his handiwork. (Psalm 19) How vast are the heavens, how mysterious the sun, moon, and stars in their circuits. How small the earth in comparison. Yet this amazing world is my home: the snow covered mountains, the powerful surge of the oceans, the springs of water high in the hills, the fish filled streams that carry the cargoes of commerce to needy people; the trees and flowers, the flowing grain and harvest, the workmen and others who feed my mind and body and promote my welfare. What in the vastness of this immense universe is man? (See Psalm 8) Yet you are mindful of him. You have

161

made me so I can share your secrets. You have made me different than all else in space and in your creation. Even I can know you and be warmed by your love. I can put my trust in you who made heaven and earth, and I can claim the quiet found in outer space and the peace of the heavens, and your love that is steadfast and true. Surely so great a God and so manifold your provisions for my life make me secure and content as I put my life in your hands and seek your quiet and peace for me this night. This comforts and quiets me.

Prayer.

Calm my mind and my spirit, O God. As I think of the wonderful ways you have brought joy and happiness to me, I place my life, and the lives of those I love in your hands, knowing that the very best that I seek for them and for myself will bring untold blessing, provided it expresses your will. I recall how often Jesus touched life at the point of its greatest need and brought peace and fullness of life. Touch me now in the quiet of this night and grant me peaceful quiet and sleep. Amen.

Doubt

Why am I so troubled? My tranquility and certainties have been invaded by questions and doubts. Some of my doubts disturb me greatly because now I am not certain about God and my life and the world about me. How can I handle these doubts that trouble me?

Was it because people questioned old wives' tales about disease that great progress was made in physical wellbeing? And was it because others questioned primitive theories about the origin of life that great mounds of evidence pointing to a long and mysterious past have been found? Was it because prophets, priests, and kings questioned the need for human sacrifice and other magic rites that they were able to broaden our spiritual understanding and our knowledge and worship of God? Once people doubted whether an object heavier than air could fly. And other technology has pushed back the frontiers of myth and magic and have gradually made humans ever more responsible for their own welfare. Even our minds and our spirits compete for a satisfactory interpretation of the meaning and purpose of life. And our very nature rebels against half truths. Could this possibly mean that had these and others not sought answers to their doubts we would still be stalking the wild boar in the jungle with intellects scarcely greater than the animals we hunted?

Could it be that my real trouble is not the questions and doubts themselves but what I permit them do to me? When I try to handle verifiable facts that contradict my earlier understanding, I let my doubts harden into negative mental postures that threaten my faith. Should I not realize that what is happening may well be the first step toward a grander view of life and of God and that this calls for a continuing search and enlargement of spirit and mind. I need to remember that every grand discovery about God and the meaning of life has passed through its valley before it reached the heights.

The answer to my doubts involves my whole being and not only my reasoning. My mental grasp is only part of life. I need insights rather than arguments. I need discernment rather than debate. I must be prepared to trust the highest my mind can project and the most stimulating my heart can hope for and then confirm or reject my findings. It is when I attempt to live within my doubts life is inhibited. It is when I probe and reach beyond my knowing there is fulfillment. I want to handle evidences from life as one great soul did when his faith was fortified by these observations: He confirmed that love is better than hate, kindness than cruelty, humility than pride, self-sacrifice than egotism, loveliness than bestiality, Jesus than Hitler, St. Francis than a playboy. This evidence makes sense. It speaks to my whole being and begins to provide a way through the maze of uncertainty.

My God is a great God. If he were so small that my mind could fully comprehend him, he would not be worthy of my worship nor would he be capable of achieving his purposes. I may never fully understand but with an eager follower of old I too can pray, "Lord I believe, help my unbelief," (Mark 9:24) and be thankful to God that he is more than able to help me handle my most perplexing doubts. I will overcome my doubts by living out my faith and God will open up ways of spiritual growth that will serve me all the days of my life.

Prayer.

In the quiet of this moment when I search for a greater understanding of my world and of my life, I need a power and a reality greater than myself. I am not fully satisfied with the faith that has been given me or my knowledge of God and of Christ. O you who has brought order and amazing wonder to your creation so that whether I search for the tiniest particle in existence or look into the vastness of space, there I see structures that defy human inventiveness or understanding. When I look at the human order and see conflict and sinfulness, I perceive that humankind has failed to mount up to the best it knows. There is need not only to probe deeper into the mysteries of your love and power, but only as I grow in faith and live out that faith can I overcome sin and remove doubt and uncertainty from my life.

I cannot be certain of the future. My mind may be unequal to the task of probing the unknown but you who have made me and have promised to guide me into all truth, now speak to me. Even as Jesus came into the dark night of the world and the darkness could not put out the light of his life, so be the light to illumine my understanding and fulfill your creation in me. Take away my doubts and open up my life to your truth, for I ask it in the name of Jesus who called his followers to one day be the light of the world. Amen.

Pain

Pain frightens me. Often when it first grips me I am terrified and am afraid I will die. Even when it seems to grow worse I still hold on. I understand there is a threshold of pain beyond which it cannot pass, and for that I am thankful. I am also thankful that there are medications that bring gratifying relief for most types of physical pain. While they lessen pain I must find a way to handle the trauma so that it does not leave me terrified and exhausted.

Now that science is providing medicines to alleviate many physical pains they are not my worst problem. The pain of the mind that comes from being misunderstood or falsely accused, or doing things I am ashamed of, or even the separation from family and friends are more disturbing. Such pains are just as real but there are no chemicals to lessen their intensity.

As if these are not enough there are pains that accompany my failures: yielding to temptation, cruel words or acts, being unwilling to take a stand, and the fear of being dishonest, unfaithful, spiteful, or in other ways failing to live up to high spiritual and moral standards. There are pains also because some of my choices make me miserable. Must I permit pain to take so much of the real joy out of life or should I be able to rid myself of its torment?

Some try drugs, including alcohol, but inevitably the temporary relief is more than offset by the devastation that follows. What appears to be an easy out does not change things. Soon the pain is back and the causes for the pain remain. Until I deal with the causes I will suffer pain.

Pains of the mind and spirit are invariably due to wrongdoing so I must rid myself of the causes and seek God's forgiveness. In this way pain can be healing. It can act as a reminder that life is getting out of hand and needs the purifying discipline that only God can give. When pain makes me dissatisfied with my moral and spiritual failures it arouses me to respond to what will contribute most to my life. I must seek God's forgiveness and guidance so this will happen.

There is another kind of pain that can contribute much to my life. When Jesus was in the Garden of Gethsemane he prayed that the cup of pain and suffering might be spared him, nevertheless not his will but God's be done. (Mt. 26:36ff) At the heart of our faith is the cross and the cross is a symbol of pain. When Jesus suffered and died on the cross he took the worst that mankind could do to him and turned it into the very best he could do for the world — to lay down his life in agonizing pain. It brought blessing and redemption to all mankind. And although Jesus suffered real pain it was swallowed up in his conscious determination to endure for the sake of others.

I probably will never be called to undergo the full intensity of such pain but I will certainly need to make painful decisions that may take from my comfort for the good of others. When that happens I pray that I may venture forth in faith, so that in some small way I may help end the suffering of others.

I must realize that sometimes it is painful to love more deeply, to feel myself part of the life of family and friends more completely, to lose myself more utterly in outgoing compassion, but such pain can be redemptive. It does not drain out goodness but gives my life a certain glory.

This poem was found written on a hospital wall.

The cry of man's anguish went up to God,
Lord, take away pain!
The shadow that darkens the world thou hast made;
The close soiling chain
That strangles the heart; the burden that weighs
On the wings that should soar —

165

Lord, take away pain from the world thou hast made
That it love you the more!

Then answered the Lord to the cry of the world,
Shall I take away pain,
And with it the power of the soul to endure,
Made strong by the strain?
Shall I take away pity that knits heart to heart;
And sacrifice high?
Will you lose all your heroes that lift from the fire
White brows to the sky?
Shall I take away love that redeems with a price
And smiles with its loss?
Can ye spare from your lives that would cling unto mine
The Christ on His cross?

Prayer.

O Lord, I seek your strength to live each day in obedience and trust. So guide and direct me that I may conquer pain with your blessing and help and in so far as it gives direction and strength to my life, to accept it gracefully and live courageously.

I pray for all those who suffer physical pain, whose hours pass slowly and whose tears of anguish in their loneliness add to their torment, wondering why freedom from their pain is so slow in coming. May their courage have the buoyancy of your grace.

Grant me forgiveness for those sins that are the cause of my pain so that I may replace evil with good. So fill my days with your steadfast love that I will engage my full powers to bring health and happiness to others and to myself. So I throw myself on your mercy, knowing that being upheld by your grace, you will do for me what is best, giving me strength and peace. In your blessed name, Amen.

Loss of a Spouse

I have lost one who has been dearer than words can tell. My breath comes laboriously. My mind is troubled. The comfort offered by relatives and friends hardly penetrates my despair. I am stunned and overcome.

Jesus, too, wept. He was at the tomb of Lazarus. The two sisters had lost their brother when Jesus was far away. Now he had come to meet their special needs. Why did he weep? He shared their sorrow. Their loss touched him deeply. He was moved with compassion. His very presence and the power of God he was to release enabled the sisters to rejoice. And now I call on the compassionate Jesus to be with me and bring me the comfort and assurance of eternal life that he revealed in his own resurrection. He shares my sorrow. I can feel his presence.

Already inner assurances begin to fortify me. I begin to think more clearly about the one who has gone from me. The glory of the life that has departed begins to rise up to mock my moment of grief. The awareness of love, of thoughtful ways, of response to my tender care, of years of planning and joyful living come rushing back to dry my tears and bring a smile of gratitude on my face. I thank God not only for the years that were so blessed but for faith and trust and hope that enriched and fulfilled our lives. I know that death is a part of God's plan for all his children and that all spirits are eternal, that while my loved one is no longer physically present, he is near in spirit and this comforts, sustains and strengthens me.

How grateful I am for family and friends who have brought such joy to both of us. All those who shared our home added their unique blessings to our lives, so I now gain strength from their goodness and I truly rejoice. Even the burdens and hardships we knew forged deeper bonds of tender love. Our common faith and outreach in love to others now add to my consolation and peace. Although our shared years were demanding they also revealed the inner strength God provides. God's steadfast love surrounded us to fortify us for all the joys and sorrows of each passing year. Jesus promised, "I will not leave you comfortless but will come to you and be with you to wipe away your tears and give you inner springs of rejoicing, welling up within you to serve you both now and for all eternity." (John 14) Because my trustworthy God is the One who has guarded us all through life I can now release my beloved to him. I feel God's tender forgiveness and mercy, his vigilant concern, at this moment. Shepherd of my soul, hear my prayer.

O thou, who has given me long years to enjoy the marvels of your world and has enlarged my heart to know the blessedness of mutual love, and for your steadfast love and faithfulness, let not the grief or loss of this moment overshadow the continuing ministry of your presence.

Never have I needed you more than at this moment. The manifold new demands that now are mine overwhelm me. Were it not that I am bold to claim your support and unfailing power as I face this moment, I would lose heart. Even as Jesus said, "Blessed are those who mourn for they shall be comforted," now I claim that comfort. Let my anxiety pass as I place my hand in yours and in full confidence know that in the days to come I may share your grander view of life and death and be fortified and uplifted by your everlasting arms so that as in the past I may be made to rejoice once more for my length of years and the blessings I have shared with the departed.

Because you have heard my voice I have been renewed in faith to be strong and full of grace and peace. My heart rejoices as you lift up my spirit and support me with your love. In the blessed name of Jesus, hear my prayer. Amen.

Before an Operation

When the doctor told me I must undergo an operation and/or take treatments to restore my health I was frightened and full of despair. How could I find the strength and wisdom I need for this new crisis? Thank God, after a brief time I got hold of myself and began to face up to what I have to do. I know that as long as there is life, there is hope. So I learned all I could about my condition and found that there were a number of options and procedures. As is true of all serious illnesses there is no absolute assurance that all will go well, but with such helpful surgeons and nurses and the prayers and love of family and friends, I have begun to get a fresh grip on myself. Now I must prepare myself so that I will not be over anxious and add to the problem but will be able to apply all my mental, spiritual, and physical energy to my recovery.

At first I asked why this had to happen to me. Is God trying to punish me for some past sin or is this happening so I will think more deeply about myself and respond to his will in a way that will greatly enrich my life? Should I throw myself on his mercy, remembering that he has said whatever we ask in his name will be done to us? What if I were to ask him to miraculously cure me? Would that be an exercise of faith or would it be telling God what he should do? Is this the way God wants to help me or has he entrusted his secrets in a special way to doctors who bring about cures as part of his plan? My faith in God tells me to place myself in his loving care and give the skilled doctors and nurses an opportunity to perform my heavenly

Father's will for my healing. How grateful I am that there are physicians, surgeons, and nurses to use their God-given skills for my good. I must prepare myself to give God right of way as I follow the regimen provided for my good.

My illness and my treatment is a very personal matter, yet it would be harmful and wrong if I were to fail to tell my dearest friends. They need to know so they can support me with their prayers and love.

My spirit is lifted as I review the many blessings of my life and recall how at times when I was about to give up I soon discovered that God had given me inner resources of faith and hope that revived and blessed me. Now I feel led of God to prepare myself and in pondering his goodness I lay claim to his promises. I will draw freely on the spiritual and physical supports God graciously supplies so they will make their maximum contribution to my recovery. He will not fail me nor forsake me. Now in his strength I am ready to face whatever is before me.

Prayer.

Look on me with your favor, O God, as I place myself in the hands of those who use their skill to bring healing and renewal. I am restless and not sure what this day may bring. Grant me quietness and courage.

Guide and bless those who attend my needs. My heart is full of gratitude for the secrets of life and health you have made known that now come to my aid. Hold me in the strong arms of faith. You who gave me life, now support me as I reach out for your continued blessing. You who heal all diseases, who redeem life from destruction, you are my keeper. You preserve my going out and my coming in day after day. Take away my anxiety. Support and strengthen me all the day long. How grateful I am that you are near to comfort and bless me now and in the days to come.

You have put in my heart tender affection for family, friends, and all those who bring comfort and love. May they be assured of my love and gratitude and bind our lives ever more closely so that we may rejoice together for your goodness.

Most of all I give thanks for the trust and faith that renews my life every day, and for the Lord, Jesus Christ, who himself suffered for my sins and my redemption, and offers to comfort and support me in every need. Accept my prayer, in his blessed name. Amen.

Anxiety

We are told not to be anxious, but this moment I am troubled. Not only am I thinking of persons and events that have caused me grief and concern in the past, but I find it hard to be composed because of today's pressures. And what tranquility I did have has been cut short as I contemplate the future. My physical strength is uncertain and provision for my essential needs gives me concern. I feel more alone because of the dwindling number of relatives, friends and those on whom I have depended. Some changes and adjustments are called for but I am not confident which way to turn. Were it not that at times when I have been sorely tested God gave me strength to rise above my difficulties, I would indeed be tempest tossed and at a loss. I reach out to you now for support. Speak to my mind and heart so that I may find a way to quiet my troubled spirit. Guide me through my present anxiety.

When Jesus said, "do not be anxious about your life, what you shall eat or what you shall drink, nor about your body what you shall put on," he did not ignore their importance. He continued. "Your heavenly Father knows that you need these things," and he assured his followers that if they got their priorities right "all these things will be yours as well." He asked them to put their trust in God and to live with assurance each day, for being anxious would not add a moment to their lives while on the other hand those who trust God and are obedient are certain to find ways to deal with their most crucial anxieties. (Mt. 6:25ff)

It may be that my situation is similar to that of St. Paul when he said that he believed that the difficulties he and his companions experienced were intended to show "the transcendent power belongs to God and not to us." So he could say, "We are afflicted in every way, but not crushed; perplexed, but not driven to despair; persecuted, but not forsaken; struck down, but not destroyed. . . . We do not lose heart. Though our outer nature is wasting away, our inner nature is being renewed day by day." (2 Cor. 4:7ff.) Some of my distress may be God's way of drawing me out of my complacency and self assurance so that I can glimpse the life I should be living.

Throughout the Bible there are stories of men and women who passed through devastating hardships. They discovered that when they put their trust in God, ways opened to them. God did not forsake them and they gained fresh insight and composure as they ventured forth in faith. According to the Psalmist God told those who passed through the valley of shadows, "I will be with you." (Ps. 23) That is comforting for he assures me that whatever may come I will not have to face my problems alone. He will help me overcome my anxieties. I will prevail as I exercise my faith and put my trust in God rather than depend on my own wisdom and strength. Often I will turn to God in prayer.

O God, I do trust you. You have reassured me that I do not have to face my anxieties and trials alone. You will lead and guide me, lift my burdens, and open up ways so I can gain control over my problems. You have called me to turn over my worries and stressful anxieties to you. You will help me meet life's needs and give me strength to accept each new demand. You will give me clearer vision and increase my wisdom so I can make right decisions. You will help me surmount each problem so I can come to grips with future necessities. You have assured me that all things are possible if I put my trust in you. Help me to do this for you are my God and Christ is my Lord, and you are able to do "far more abundantly than all that I ask or think." (Ephesians 3:20) Thanks be to God and to Christ my Lord, that through faith and trust I can shake off my anxieties and look to the future with assurance and joyful obedience. Amen.

Guilt

At times my tranquility and peace of mind is sorely troubled by a feeling of guilt that simply does not go away. Now, at this time of life, when I have more time to think and should gain immeasurably from past experiences, my mind dredges up those indiscretions, mistakes, sins, that I thought had been forgiven and they torment me. I must find ways to handle this obsession.

My Guilt interferes with so much of life. It separates me from some who could add immeasurably to the fullness of life I am so eager to have. And if I do not rightly handle my guilt I may push it down into my subconscious where it can issue forth in painful illnesses, complexes, or mental disturbance that might become uncontrollable. I long to be free of both the open and suppressed guilt that troubles me.

It weighs heavily on my mind that I failed to fulfill the dreams of my youth. When I think more clearly about this I realize that most of the time I acted the best I could under the circumstances. Even now I am not perfect. It would help me greatly if I could accept myself, limitations and all, cease dwelling on my failures, and rejoice that God has guided me and led me to achieve as much as I have. Rather than blame myself unduly I should remember that even such a spiritual giant as the apostle Peter denied knowing his Lord at the trial, then he went out and wept bitterly. Afterwards Peter got rid of his guilt and became one of the founders of Christianity. I will ask God to rid me of my guilt.

Jesus on a number of occasions told how forgiveness sets a person free. To the woman caught in adultery, who faced death by her accusers, Jesus offered forgiveness and told her to go and sin no more. He said to her accusers, whoever of you is without sin, cast the first stone, and they dropped their stones and fled. We do not know what happened to the girl but he not only forgave her but offered her a new life if she would sin no more.

Again, Jesus told the story of the Prodigal Son. The boy sowed his wild oats and was destitute. The moment of change came when the boy said, "I will arise and go to my father and say, I have sinned against heaven and earth, make me as a hired servant." And when his father saw him coming he ran to meet him and said, "My son was dead and is alive. He was lost and is found." That father, and Jesus identified him with his Heavenly Father, forgave the boy and restored him to his family and his home.

Forgiveness does more than wipe away the feeling of guilt. It amounts to a new lease on life. When Jesus went to the sophisticated Nicodemus he told him that his new faith could wipe his slate clean, that the Spirit of God would so reshape his life that it was like being born again — a fresh start under the inspiration of God's Spirit. God is ready to do that for me, too.

This now becomes clear. Whatever has happened in the past needs not continue to haunt me. I can turn it all over to God. He does not want to take away the joy of my remaining years but to forgive me so that by putting those things behind I can live out my days drawing on his steadfast love, his grace. This must be what St. Paul meant when he said, "forgetting what lies behind and straining forward to ⸱t lies ahead, I press on toward the goal for the prize of the ᵈ call of God in Christ Jesus." (Phil. 3:13f.) This is possible for me, too. With God's forgiveness I will be free of guilt and able to live the rest of my days knowing his peace and joy.

Prayer.

O God, I seek your forgiveness. I lay my hates, my injustices, my wrongdoing before you. Forgive me for the wrong I have done. My guilt has taken away from the fullness of life you would have me know. Release in me your Spirit that I may be more loving, more eager to serve others, more full of life. Because you offer forgiveness I begin to feel like a new person, like the healed leper Jesus told of whose faith made him whole. (Luke 17:19) My self-pity, my evasion of responsibility, my fear of consequences are gone. I begin to realize what the Psalmist meant when he said, "Blessed is he whose transgression is forgiven, whose sin is covered." (Ps. 32:1) Now a new life stretches out before me, larger and more a part of your divine plan. Grant me your favor so that from this day I may pass on to others the blessings that are even now giving me newness of life. Thank you, my heavenly Father, that you have broken the shackles of guilt and have made me whole again. My Jesus, you have clearly pointed the way. Now walk with me and fill my life with your compassionate Spirit, for I pray in your blessed name. Amen.

Approaching Death

There comes a time when signals from my body tell me that I do not have long to live. One can never be entirely ready for an extraordinary change and especially such a one as this. However I have been told that death, itself, is not to be feared, rather as the end approaches there is almost always complete calm and a readiness that is not anticipated but is completely peaceful.

Now I want to put final things in order. As I have passed through life I have found a Source that has sustained me in every threatening experience. Such experiences have shown me that because of God's steadfast love, he has endowed me with inner resources and strength that have uplifted the good and turned away sin. Because I have felt the tug of eternity on my heart throughout life God has released redemptive acts and experiences all my days. God is no stranger to me and because of the measure of my faith, he has endowed me with courage and hope as I make the final passage, and he will add lustre and benediction as long as I have breath.

The words of Jesus comfort me, "I am the resurrection and the life: he that believeth in me shall never die but shall have everlasting life." There is comfort to feel Jesus near now that my days on earth are brief. I have been glad to accept life as a gift and you have blessed me. Now I lay it down. Accept my grateful thanks for the joys and wonders of past years.

Even as life itself is a mystery so is death. Many have tried to describe what it will be like. It is enough to know that the same loving God who has sustained me these years also rules the land to which my soul will go. So all fear of death gives way to a sense of wonder and joy as a new life begins; a life that will be fairer and more satisfying than all that I have known.

The welcome I give death may bring more comfort to me than it does to those I love and who have so faithfully cared for me. Loving thoughts fill my heart for doctors and nurses, family and friends, for shepherds of my soul and all those who have added stature and glory to my life; for schools and churches, and those of kindred mind who sought to lighten the burdens of others. Even as I glorify your name for these and others who have touched my life and brought me to this hour, I am aware that your hand has guided me and into your hands I can gratefully and contentedly put my soul for all eternity. There may be some sadness of farewell as there is in every parting, but may the glory of our lives and the strength of our faith sweep away our tears as this new life begins, greater far than our earthly pilgrimage and eternal in the heavens forevermore.

Prayer.

My heavenly Father, even as in life I did commit myself to your loving care, so now awaiting death I claim your promises of steadfast, enduring, eternal love. I know from Jesus that death is not the end but a new beginning and that it does not take me out of my Father's hands nor separate me from the love of God. Make firm my faith in Christ and then I shall have the peace of Christ.

You have made me know redemption and fullness of life. You have offered to forgive my sins as I have forgiven the sins of others. Take away all that is impure. Free me from the sense of guilt for my forgiven failures. Cleanse my mind and my heart as I claim the blessings that are promised through Christ my Lord.

Make strong my last days upon earth: strong in faith, full in love, grateful and helpful in response to all that is done for my comfort and release. Earnestly and in true confidence I pray and may the blessed peace that I now feel support and uplift all those who are drawn into the circle of my love, both now and for all eternity. Amen.

It Is Up To You

You are not so much threatened by what happens on the outside as by your tensions and stresses on the inside. The more alive you are and the more you are engaged in life-support activities, the greater will be your need for spiritual resources adequate to control or dissipate your tensions.

The following are steps you can take to discover and utilize all God wants to do for you.

1. Prayer and meditation. Learn to open your heart to God. Set aside regular periods daily for scripture reading, prayer, and waiting to hear God speak to you. Then never wander far from the Source of your life. Make it a habit to ask for reinforced strength in body and mind at any moment of need and especially when you feel vulnerable. Meditate on the compassionate Jesus and he will touch your life as he touched so many long ago and you will know healing as you accept God's will for your life.

2. Put your faith to work. Faith is counting on God to help you. Know that even as God gave his Son that you might have life and have it abundantly, he has made your body and mind not to be tormented and defeated but to meet every stress and difficulty in his strength. Some trials come as testings needed to fortify and develop your inner strength. Not all illnesses or tensions will be removed but they may become stepping stones for inner illumination.

Faith is not a passive acceptance of your condition. Turn faith into a verb and make it faithing. In faith act out the positive response to your condition. No longer let the physical or mental enemy hold you in its grip. Not only think positive thoughts, act them out. When John Wesley complained that he did not have faith, he was advised, begin to act out your faith and very soon your faith will take over, then you will act because of your faith.

3. Gain the loving support of others. The community of the

175

faithful include nurses, clergymen, family, friends, and others whose lives will be enriched as you touch their heartstrings by sharing your burden. Both you and the circle of devout souls who hold you in their hearts will grow in the knowledge and love of God. It is not always easy to confide in others but this may be your most rewarding adventure on the way to healing.

4. Affirm confidence in your ability with divine help to resolve your difficulty. Do not blame others nor attribute your problems to the devil. The devil is powerless in the presence of God's Holy Spirit who is ever present to meet your needs. Do not evade responsibility by laying blame on any power outside yourself. Be determined to overcome evil with good, following St. Paul's advice. In God's strength your stumbling blocks will be turned into stepping stones. Even in those instances when you may not be healed, you will be given spiritual strength that will sustain you. And you will be enlarged and made whole as you courageously confront your difficulty with God's help.

5. Share your faith. Do not hide the light of your life under a bushel. Be involved and active in ways that help others meet their problems even though your condition may make it impossible to do more than reach out in warm friendship to others. Your anguish of soul will equip you to be compassionate and helpful and this will speed your own recovery and help turn your trials into triumphs. Try it. You will become someone's clear evidence of God at work in today's perplexing world.

ACKNOWLEDGEMENTS

Long ago a sage concluded, "there is nothing new under the sun." (Ecclesiastes 1:9c) All that comes to us to enrich our minds comes through hearing, seeing, or feeling. Then, after we have meditated and pondered on these impressions, we pass on to others whatever has deeply inspired us.

As I think of the many sources behind these meditations, I find it impossible to remember the origin of all I have written. This is a difficulty common to many ministers, for it becomes his (or her) particular privilege to search out the wisdom of the ages, and after reflecting on it, to give it fresh utterance. Often it takes on an aura of a new discovery released so forcefully it lifts the spiritual understanding of his generation. I found this true of such a man as John Wesley. As I applied myself to extract his theology from his letters, diary, sermons, and edited works, I observed how his alert mind lifted up wisdom, hoary with age, and proclaimed it in strickingly new and seemingly original utterances, and in doing so his ministry was all the more effective.

It was not so customary in Wesley's day to credit sources. But it is as true now as it was then that at best a minister is able to identify, for certain, only a few of the insights he shares with others. The very fact that he is eager to share them, speaks of his respect and gratitude for the ones who have enlightened him.

I find it impossible to acknowledge all from whom I have drawn directly or indirectly. I have gained so much from so many. My father was a minister, and his ministry is reflected here. Kindly teachers, professors, colleagues, other ministers, innumerable authors, and the named and unnamed writers who left their spiritual discoveries in holy writ, are among those I should mention. I have discovered truth in many unexpected places, from the humble peasant of India to such an inspired soul as Mahatma Gandhi. How, then, does one write an acknowledgement?

There are in these meditations, lines I owe to a definite source. Some I can identify and gratefully acknowledge in the notes that

177

follow. Some among them have given me permission to use information from their sources and you will join me in thanking them. But the origin of some references and information is lost to me, in spite of long hours of research. It has not been my intention to overlook any known source. My prayer would be that you who read these pages will acknowlege with me our common debt to both those I identify and those who remain unnamed. May the inspiration I have felt filter through to you who read these meditations.

Among those who have contributed in a special way to the preparation of this work are my wife, who has given her continued support to the undertaking and has done much of the proofreading and Mary E. Batchelor for her editorial assistance. The Reverend Thomas C. Cook, Jr., of the National Interfaith Coalition on Aging, brought the encouragement of his organization to the completion of this project, and had it not been for the continued encouragement and guidance of Dr. Richard T. Conard, President of Southmark Foundation on Gerontology, the writing of these meditations would have remained only a prospect. While being grateful for this and other assistance he has had, the author in writing these meditations, has given expression to his own cherished thoughts which are the fruit of a life-long quest for truth and many years of exceptional experiences. Now we are able to release this book with the hope it will add to the spiritual welfare of many.

NOTES

*(The reference numbers below refer to pages in the Meditations)

The hymns found in the Meditations are from the *Methodist Hymnal*, Nashville, The Methodist Publishing House, 1939.

The scripture quotations are from the Revised Standard Version of the Bible, copyrighted 1946, 1952, (c) 1971, 1973, The Division of Education and Ministry of the National Council of Churches, New York, and used with permission.

2 Walter Dudley Cavert, *Remember Now*, Nashville, Abingdon Press, 1944. Orpheus, p. 60.

6 Anne Morrow Lindbergh, as quoted by Halford E. Luccock in *365 Windows*, Nashville, The Abingdon Press, (c) 1965...1970, p. 198.

11 The poem, "Windows of the Soul," author unknown, is quoted by Merton S. Rice, *Diagnosing Today*, Nashville, Abingdon Press, 1932.

14 The reference to Brother Lawrence, from the *Practicing of the Presence of God*, being conversations and letters of Nicholas Herman of Lorraine, translated from the French, and found in various sources, among which is the booklet published by Fleming H. Revell Co., Westwood, New Jersey. Among Brother Lawrence's utterances, we note in particular these: "The time of business does not with me differ from the time of prayer," and, "...in the noise and clatter of my kitchen...I possess God in as great tranquility as if I were upon my knees at the blessed sacrament."

14 The portion of the poem "Renascence," by Edna St. Vincent Millay is found in her *Collected Poems*, Harper and Row, 1917, 1945, and used with permission of Norma Millay Ellis.

17 The reference to Thomas Gray and George Eliot, from Luccock, *Op. Cit.*, p. 117.

17 A sermon by Dr. Norman Vincent Peale, "Peace for a Troubled Mind," Creative Help for Daily Living., Vol. 31, No. 6, part II, May 22, 1977, The Foundation for Christian Living, Pawling, New York, and used with permission.

21 From Albert Schweitzer, *A Quest for the Historical Jesus*.

22 The description of love by St. Augustine may be found in *The Guideposts Treasury of Faith*, Guidepost's Magazine, 1970.

25 William L. Stidger's story of Sadie Virginia Smithson, from his book, *There are Sermons in Stories*, Nashville, Abingdon Press, 1942, pp. 11f.

41 The quotation from Abraham Lincoln is found in Arthur Gordon, *A Touch of Wonder*, New York, Guideposts Associates, 1974, Fleming H. Revell Co., p. 93.

43 The story of Orville Kelley was told by Howard L. Rosenberg, "Dying, He Makes Every Day Count," The Parade Publications, New York, 1980. Used with permission of Parade Publications and Howard L. Rosenberg.

46 Russel R. Conwell, *Acres of Diamonds*, Harper and Brothers, 1915. People in India associate the famous Kohinoor and Orloff diamonds with the historically famous Glocanda Diamond Market located just outside the city of Hyderabad, Deccan, in south central India. The Market was a part of the famous fort that still stands, though now largely a crumbling landmark. That Golconda is 1500 miles from the Indus River which flows near Hyderabad, Sindh. Apparently there is some question about the actual locale of the story.

52 Stidger, *Op. Cit.* pp. 226f.

179

57   The description of the woman actor in London is told by Will and Ariel Durant, *The Story of Civilization*, Vol. VIII, p. 274, New York: Simon and Schuster, 1963.

59   John Ruskin's comments about the lamplighter are found in various sources. The one reported here by Ralph L. Wood is from *The Guideposts Treasury of Faith, Op. Cit.*

69   For this portion of the poem "Renascence," see Edna St. Vincent Millay, *Op. Cit.*

71   For an excellent study of Jonah, see William M. Pickering *rather die than live—Jonah*, Education and Cultivation Division, Board of Global Ministries, The United Methodist Church, New York, 1974.

74   Dr. Albert Caliandro, "What to Do When Life Says No?" See Creative Help for Daily Living, part III, Vol. 28, No. 6, 1977, Foundation for Christian Living, Pawling, New York. Used with permission.

77   The story behind Dürer's famous painting, The Praying Hands, is told by Cynthia Pearl Maus, *Christ and the Fine Arts*, Harper Brothers, 1938.

80   Dr. Harry Emerson Fosdick, *The Manhood of the Master*, (c) 1921, by Association Press, and used with permission of Follet Publishing Co.

83   Stidger, *Op. Cit.*, p. 130, for the woman who was declared beautiful.

92   Albert Schweitzer, *Out of My Life and Thought*, translated by C. T. Campion, copyright 1933, 1949, (c) 1961, 1977 by Holt, Rinehart and Winston and used with the permission of the publishers.

93   Luccock, *Op. Cit.* p. 14. Dr. Conant's turtle.

93   Edwin Markham's poem, "Live and Help Live," is printed in numerous books of poems.

96   Stidger, *Op. Cit.* pp. 158ff.

101   Dr. Norman Vincent Peale, "Live With Yourself and Enjoy Yourself," Creative Helps for Daily Living, September 1979, pp. 4, 6f. Foundation for Christian Living. Used with permission.

102   For the reference to Charles Darwin and Abraham Lincoln, see Thomas S. Kepler, *Leaves From a Spiritual Notebook*, (c) 1960, Nashville, Abingdon Press and used with permission.

110   Halford E. Luccock, *Op. Cit.* p. 104.

112   Roy H. Stetler, *With God We Can*, Harrisburg, Pa., The Evangelical Press, 1958, for an imaginary trip to Jerusalem, p. 72.

119   Kepler, *Op. Cit.* p. 108, for the experience of Rufus Jones.

123   Stidger, *Op. Cit.*, pp 156ff.

127   Walter Dudley Cavert, *Ours Is The Faith*, Nashville, Abingdon Press, (c) 1960, tells of Robert Raikes, pp. 248f.

129   J. B. Phillips, translator, *The New Testament in Modern English*, Revised Edition, (c) J. B. Phillips, 1958, 1960, 1972.

134   Luccock, *365 Windows, Op. Cit.* p. 22. Is the sermon ended?

140   Luccock, *Ibid*, p. 98.

141   Cavert, *Remember Now, Op. Cit.* p. 77.

148   Isaac Watts, When I survey the Wondrous Cross.

150   Charles L. Wallis, editor, *Lenten Easter Source Book*, Nashville, Abingdon Press, 1961. p. 99. Talmadge C. Johnson.